SESSIONS WITH CORINTHIANS

Acknowledgments

To Lisa, Mallory, and Jake . . . once again for the patience and grace provided for the research, teaching, and writing of this book.

To Kris Peters, Assistant Extraordinaire . . . for her editorial and management assistance. Cheers!

To the research library staff at the Bodleian Library, Oxford, and the University of Wales, Cardiff . . . for letting me in!

To Johns Creek Baptist Church . . . for opening the door to creativity and new ideas for adult Sunday school.

To the "brain trust" of Smyth & Helwys . . . for having the vision for a new series such as this.

Sessions *with*
Corinthians

Lessons *for the* Imperfect

Michael D. McCullar

SMYTH&HELWYS
PUBLISHING INCORPORATED · MACON, GEORGIA

Smyth & Helwys Publishing, Inc.
6316 Peake Road
Macon, Georgia 31210-3960
1-800-747-3016
©2004 by Smyth & Helwys Publishing
All rights reserved.
Printed in the United States of America.

The paper used in this publication meets the minimum requirements of
American National Standard for Information Sciences—
Permanence of Paper for Printed Library Materials.
ANSI Z39.48–1984. (alk. paper)

Library of Congress Cataloging-in-Publication Data

McCullar, Michael, 1954-
Sessions with 1 & 2 Corinthians /
by Michael McCullar.
p. cm.
ISBN 1-57312-430-3 (pbk. : alk. paper)
1. Bible. N.T.
Corinthians--Criticism, interpretation, etc.
I. Title:
Sessions with first and second Corinthians.
II. Title.
BS2675.52.M33 2004
227'.2'0071--dcc22

2004004158

Table of Contents

Sessions with Corinthians

Sessions with Corinthians is a ten-session study unit designed to provide insight into two of Paul's most important letters. Within these truly "opposite" letters one will find foundational teachings on Christian service, unity, worship, conduct, marriage, spiritual gifts and the exercise of love as a basis for living. In 2 Corinthians one will experience Paul's most personal writing and encounter his theology embedded in virtually every verse.

The genuine beauty of studying these two uniquely different letters together is to be found in Paul's focus upon the centrality of God's love. In the first letter God's love is taught through the need for proper action, while in the second letter Paul personally demonstrates his love through patience and compassion to the troubled Corinthian church. This is no doubt the best back-to-back treatise on complete faith development and practice in scripture.

Resource Pages

Sessions with Corinthians is designed for personal study, for use in classes and seminars, and as a preaching guide. Each session is followed by resource pages with several questions. Use the resource pages to allow for a deeper exploration of 1 & 2 Corinthians. The resource pages may also be used by seminar leaders and teachers as facilitation points in session preparation.

Introducing 1 & 2 Corinthians

It has been said that James is the New Testament book most applicable to day-to-day faith living. If this is true, the Corinthian letters serve the opposite purpose. The letters of Paul to the church in Corinth are filled with discord, petty thinking, rivalry, deviant sexuality, gross inequalities, and drunken communion services. These are definitely not the type of reports churches would enjoy receiving, but they do aptly describe the first century church in Corinth.

We can learn much from the problems and issues found in these letters. The universal church benefits greatly from Paul's bold stand and, in the end, the willingness of the Corinthian leaders to accept his teachings. All churches have problems, obviously some more so than others. The key to long-term church success is to learn from problems and mistakes and not to repeat them in the future. First and Second Corinthians provide us with a host of problems, issues, and mistakes from which we can learn and grow.

The City of Corinth

Corinth was captured by Rome in 146 BC and completely destroyed. The area lay in waste for more than 100 years until Julius Caesar decreed it to be rebuilt in 44 BC. Due to its unique and advantageous location, it quickly became a commercial boon for Rome. Corinth was located on an isthmus adjacent to the Adriatic and Aegean Seas. This strategic layout made east-west sea travel easy and provided for a commercially rich economic base. Over time, "Corinth grew to become the third most important city in the Roman Empire after Rome and Alexandria" (Coleman & Reace, 9).

The Culture of Corinth

History teaches that the Corinth of Paul's day was a cosmopolitan center for empire-wide commerce. Talbert cites the following for the bulk of Corinth's wealth: "Trade, travel, banking, bronze making and from the Isthmian games held every two years" (4). Due to the cosmopolitan culture of the city, it was home to many peoples and to many religions. Corinth was famous for shrines and temples to Poseidon, Apollo, Athena, Hera, Hercules, Jupiter, Isis, and Aphrodite. Worship of Aphrodite, the Goddess of Love, was said to have 1,000 prostitutes in service to the temple.

Religion was pervasive in Corinth, due mainly to the aforementioned Greek practices and to those unique to the empire. The abundance of pagan outlets provided both Judaism and the new church with many obstacles. Claman puts it this way: "Judaism and Christianity existed as minorities in a sea of pagan Roman beliefs, as well as other Eastern religions" (25).

The diverse landscape of religions and people groups also led to loose social and cultural morals. To *Corinthianize* was a common term of the day meaning to engage in immoral sexual practices. This no doubt was strengthened by the sexual practices involved in worship and service to the many pagan deities. In describing the vice and licentious behavior, Gordon Fee writes that Corinth was "the New York, Los Angeles and Las Vegas of the ancient world" (3).

Author & Date

There is great unity in declaring Paul as the author of both Corinthian letters. It is also easier to assign dates to these writings in relation to other New Testament letters. "First Corinthians was written in the third missionary journey from Ephesus and in the spring of AD 55 and 2 Corinthians may be placed in the fall of AD 56" (Gaebelein, 180). A lengthy stay by Paul in Corinth predates both letters as he helped found the church (AD 49–51).

Occasion of the Letters

First Corinthians was written in response to reports and letters received from Chloe's household (1:11). The news from Corinth was not good, as several members were having difficulty breaking with their past practices. The church was fractious and was seemingly choosing sides over the most prominent faith leaders of the day. There was also an overall quarrelsome attitude, both within the church and toward Paul. The letter Paul received from Corinthian church leaders is thought to have contained certain questions and focused on specific issues. Paul's framework in 1 Corinthians seems designed as a response to specific instances, issues, and questions.

The second Corinthian letter is crafted much differently than the earlier one. A rising level of resistance and antagonism toward Paul is evident in the tone of the second letter. The bulk of 2 Corinthians deals with Paul's defense of his ministry, of his apostolic authority, and of his theology.

It is believed Paul wrote four letters to the Corinthian church. The first letter would have preceded the scriptural first letter and is referred to in 1 Corinthians 5:9-10. A third letter is often called the "severe letter" and is referred to in 2 Corinthians 7:8-9. Both the actual first letter and the third or middle letter between our 1 & 2 Corinthians are lost. There are scholars who believe the "severe letter" was added to the end of 2 Corinthians at a later date, if not in whole, at least in part.

There seems to be little disagreement over 2 Corinthians being the body of Paul's work that is most difficult to understand. This is due in no small part to the aforementioned belief that the second letter is most likely multiple letters, but also due to the obvious stained relationship between Paul and the Corinthian church. It is difficult to estimate the amount of ill will in place surrounding the occasion of the other letters. From the point of Paul's departure, after one and a half years, both the church and their views of Paul regressed greatly. The final letter(s) play out against this backdrop.

"Where to start?" Paul must have faced this dilemma as he set out to address the questions and issues plaguing the struggling church in Corinth. Disunity is a root disease that over time can literally destroy both the vitality and function of a church. Possibly no other single issue can impact the life and health of a fellowship of believers as this one can. New Testament churches are to be unified in purpose, thought, and love, projecting their "togetherness" to an already fractionalized world. Divided churches are their own worst enemies. How many "yet-to-be reached" people actually want to add to the chaos of their lives by linking with a fractured church?

The Corinthian Symptom

Now I appeal to you, brothers and sisters, by the name of our Lord Jesus Christ, that all of you be in agreement and that there be no divisions among you, but that you be united in the same mind and the same purpose. (1 Cor 1:10)

Modern-day Republicans and Democrats have nothing on the mid-first century Christians in Corinth when it comes to partisan politics. For a small, relatively new group, these Christians were divided into an amazing number of camps. The biblical ideal is to be of "one mind" as Paul writes, but in reality there were multiple minds and opinions in play.

In Corinth there was a natural state of unease between Gentiles and Jewish converts. It was not uncommon in the first-century church for Hebrew believers to view Gentiles as spiritually inferior. There is no doubt that the Gentile Christians lacked the historical and traditional faith experience enjoyed by Hebrew believers.

However, this friction was not the worst display of disunity within this church. Paul's focus was on the splitting up into parties of preference based on the leadership of actual people. "There were four parties or rival factions in the Corinthian Church—a Paul Party, an Apollos party, a Cephas (Peter) party, and a Christ Party" (Dunn, 28).

Anyone who has ever played kickball knows that dividing into teams is a natural part of life. The church, however, is the one facet of life where any such division is counterproductive, even pernicious. Failure is the common result for a divided church, and that was the probable looming destiny for the Corinthians if their disunity remained or progressed.

Parties & Factions

The church had lapsed into taking sides by person—some opting for Paul, others for Apollos, Peter, or Jesus. We will never know the exact reasons for these splits of preference. They did exist, however, and seemed firmly entrenched to the point of creating distinct camps within the church. It is possible that those who opted for Paul had viewed his labor in the founding of the church or had heard of his miraculous salvation experience. The Apollos group was likely drawn by Apollos's oratory skills and intelligence (Acts 18:21). The Peter reference is uniquely puzzling since there is no conclusive evidence that he served in Corinth. He was known to have traveled with his wife and could have visited Corinth at some point. It is also possible that his service with Jesus and success at Pentecost led to a form of fame among early believers.

The Christ group most likely represented those who saw themselves as "super spiritual" due to special blessings or unique insight. It was common for those who had seen Jesus in person to cite superiority in belief, faith, and relationship. This was especially true of Hebrew Christians who accepted Jesus' Messiahship during his earthly ministry. It's easy to see how the self-centered views of this group could have led to discord and division within the church.

Teaching the Corinthians How to Be Wise

Paul's approach to these divisions within the Corinthian church was to begin with the issue of wisdom. The root problem in the church was not their preference of leader or personality; rather it was their lack of supernatural wisdom. The Corinthians had been greatly influenced by classic, rational Greek thought. They were naturally inquisitive, logical thinkers who sought proof on all issues of consequence. This was also true of many Hebrews who had become Greek-like in thought and action due to time spent in Greece and elsewhere in the Roman Empire.

Paul goes on the defensive by simultaneously utilizing and then destroying the use of logic and reason applied to faith in Christ. "Has Christ been divided?" was an illogical picture that forced the Corinthians to see their error in intellectual ways. For a rational, logical thinker, the very thought of a divided person would be ludicrous, which was, of course, Paul's intent from the beginning. Even the Corinthian Christians were familiar with the unique link between the One Christ and the church. Beginning with Christ and extending through Pentecost, the theme of oneness and unity was prevalent. Just as one Christ could not be divided, neither should the church bearing his name be divided. In essence, they are one and the same in all ways spiritual.

> The grounds of our allegiance to Christ, are first, that he is the Christ, the Son of the Living God; second, that He has redeemed us; third, that we are consecrated to Him in baptism. All these grounds are unique to Christ. To no other being in the universe do believers stand in the relationship that they all sustain to their common Lord. As, therefore, there is but one Christ, one Redeemer, one Baptism, Christ cannot be divided without violating the bond that binds them to Christ and to one another (Hodge, 33).

Paul goes on to ask, "Was Paul crucified for you?" No doubt by this second question the Corinthians were saying, "No more, we give up, we get the point!" This question would, however, quickly strike at the center of misplaced priorities. Jesus the Messiah was crucified. Paul the supreme church planter and evangelist was merely a messenger. By invoking the crucifixion of Jesus, Paul reinforced the true uniqueness of Jesus Christ.

The Cure

No epidemic has ever been eradicated without first knowing the source of infection. Find the source and you have an opportunity to create a cure or, at the very least, to stop the spread of infection. The same line of thought could be applied to the Corinthian disease.

The symptoms were manifested by disunity, but the source was clearly inferior spirituality. They were far too human in the ways they approached wisdom and faith. They attempted to apply natural wisdom to supernatural issues. God however, had turned natural wisdom upside down through Jesus and the cross.

In vv. 23-24 Paul cites "Christ crucified, a stumbling block to Jews and foolishness to Gentiles." The Jews had hoped for a Messiah on the order of David. They sought a Messiah of power and might to lead them against Rome in ways both political and military. The Gentiles saw Jesus' death on the cross as extreme weakness and the resurrection as an impossibility. Simply put, only rank criminals die on crosses, and they do not come back to life. So while Paul described Jews and Gentiles who still dismissed Jesus as Messiah, he correctly described their overall tendencies of relying on traditional logic and rational thought.

Step 1: The first step in overcoming disunity is to move away from finite natural wisdom and utilize the gift of supernatural wisdom supplied by the Holy Spirit. James described the two types of wisdom in 3:13-16: "Who is wise and understanding among you? Let him show it by his good life, by deeds done in humility that comes from wisdom. But if you harbor bitter envy and selfish ambition in your hearts, do not boast about it or deny the truth. Such 'wisdom' does not come from heaven but is earthy, unspiritual, of the devil. For where you have envy and selfish ambition, there you find disorder and every evil practice."

James goes on to say that supernatural wisdom is pure and is of God. So we have both Paul and James drawing a line between natural human wisdom and wisdom provided by God through the Holy Spirit. The differences are clear. Faith fueled by natural wisdom leads to dysfunction; supernatural wisdom leads to righteousness. This distinction is clear and is consistently taught throughout the New Testament.

Barrett sees Paul's wisdom as "more than a wise plan; wisdom is not merely the plan but the 'stuff of salvation'" (56). The wisdom provided by God through the Holy Spirit is central to all of our faith thoughts and practices. It becomes the lens through which all else is viewed. It is difficult to default back to natural wisdom when viewing life though the lens of salvation and God's purposes.

Step 2 : The subsequent next step is to practice unity. It is obvious that humankind isn't naturally prone to unity. In fact, the exact opposite would be closer to reality. It is possible, however, for Christians to unify and be like-minded. A word study reveals that Paul seeks unity on the big issues of faith. Barrett writes, "that you may all be agreed in what you say means literally, '*that you may all say the same thing*'" (41).

The divisive issues were squarely major faith issues. Paul stresses the need to "think" alike on the major issues of faith. Another approach would be that there are certain absolutes integral to Christianity. Christians, especially those within a church, must be like-minded in regard to these absolute beliefs if they are to move in God's appointed direction. it is obvious that Christians will not agree on all aspects of faith. Paul knew this and only expected the Corinthians to agree on the absolutes.

Life Lessons

As you will note on your journey through 1 and 2 Corinthians, there is a great deal to learn from the dysfunction and error of the church of Corinth. Chapter 1 provides insight into two potential problems that continue to plague churches. First, we must focus on Jesus and not on the personality delivering the message. Far too many churches have seen the destructive result of people worshiping the messenger rather than the central focus of the message. Christ crucified, risen, and ascended is the foundation for our existence as Christians. If believers move away from that single focus, dysfunction will certainly follow. If on his best day Paul was merely a messenger, then all preachers and teachers should only aspire to the same goal.

Second, believers must tap into supernatural wisdom if God's will and purposes are to be known. There is little room within the life of a Christian for conventional, natural wisdom. That approach to decision making is flawed, temporal, and finite. It is only through the gift of spirit-wisdom that one can know what God purposes for life. Spirit-wisdom is the path to righteousness; natural wisdom is the slippery slope to all sorts of dysfunction, including disunity on a grand scale.

1. Identify ways disunity can damage, even destroy the effectiveness of a church.

_____
_____
_____
_____
_____
_____

2. What are the dangers of following individual church leaders to the point of factions forming?

_____
_____
_____
_____
_____
_____

3. Identify ways in which "inferior spirituality" plays into church disunity.

_____
_____
_____
_____
_____
_____

4. Identify ways people utilize natural wisdom rather than supernatural wisdom through the Holy Spirit.

_____
_____
_____
_____
_____

5. Briefly describe Jesus being a stumbling block to the Jews and foolishness to the Greeks (Gentiles).

_____

_____

_____

_____

_____

6. Identify the "absolutes" on which Paul seems to say all believers must agree.

_____

_____

_____

_____

_____

_____

7. If believers utilize spiritual wisdom as the lens through which life is viewed, how might life change for them as individuals? As a church?

_____

_____

_____

_____

_____

_____

8. Identify ways church disunity has led people who aren't Christians away from the faith.

_____

_____

_____

_____

_____

One Bad Apple

There are problems and then there are *problems*. Chapter five deals with the latter type of problem, one that singly depicts the depth of dysfunction within the Corinthian church. It had been brought to Paul's attention that a man in the fellowship was having a sexual relationship with his father's wife. It is easy to do a quick read of these verses and think incest and see red flags raised at the very thought of that possibility. That would be a mistake, however, since the scriptural text clearly doesn't describe the woman as the man's mother. It was no doubt his stepmother, someone his father married after the divorce or death of his birth mother. This fact doesn't improve on the dark situation a great deal, but it could have been worse.

Paul easily could have majored on the sexual sin and tutored the church on moral purity. Instead he moved quickly past the overt sin of the member to the response of the full church to the offense. Then he dealt with the community effect of sin and how the community of faith should deal with such matters.

Does Paul minimize the gross sin of the man in the process of teaching the larger church a greater lesson? No. In fact, he was harsh in his counsel on what to do with the immoral man. Paul demonstrated that both the sexual sin and the Christian response were wrong. His larger concern was the danger of rampant sin on the larger community of believers. In the "one bad apple" line of thinking, one unrepentant sinner left unchecked could pollute the entire church and derail God's purposes for and through the church.

The Sin

It is possible that worse sexual sins are dealt with in the Bible, but it is hard to find an example described as nastily as this one. The word for sexual sin in Greek is *porneia*, the root word for today's *pornography*. Let's face it, though—pornography has lost much of its onus in the past few decades. With the "anything goes" freedom of today's mass media, pornography doesn't have the reverse clout it once held. It is best to remember that this man chose to have an affair with his stepmother, a choice Paul describes as being too vile for even the average Roman pagan. Fisk comments,

> If most of the nasty details are lost to us, three points are not. First, this wife was not the man's birth mother, but a subsequent wife of his father. Second, she was not part of the church (for Paul has nothing to say about her). Third, the son and stepmother were involved sexually (the Greek word translated "has" or "living with" is a loaded term). Sophocles called it "unquessed shame." Moses calls this sin an "abomination." As for Paul, he caustically points out that this sort of corruption was "not found even among pagans" (NSRV: 5:16). (24)

Hebrew Law expressly forbade this type of sexual sin (Lev 18:8), but the strict Old Testament law was not applicable in the Christian church. Paul therefore could not formulate a corrective response based upon the law. Matters such as this became much more complicated after the perfunctory law gave way to a relationship-based (man to God) code of conduct. The quandary became even more bizarre due to the lackadaisical mind-set of the larger church body.

The Church Response

The church response to this obviously well-known liaison was, well, nothing. Their response was an awful non-response. They knew the relationship was taking place but were passive in their approach to both the sin and the sinner. Was a form of arrogance in place among the church members, or were they functionally ignorant about what to do? We must not forget that more Gentiles than Jews had faith in Christ and thus a great amount of former pagan baggage entered into the new movement. Pagan society has been historically lax on sexual morals. Fee quotes a famous line of Demos: "Mistresses we keep for the sake of pleasure, concubines for the daily care of the body, but wives to bear us legitimate children" (196). Many former pagans did not accept easily the evolved Hebrew moral restrictions on sexuality.

Fee asks the question, "Are the members arrogant in spite of what is going on among them, or because of it?" (196). Paul's condemnation of their pride in 5:2 adds to the probability that many in the church knew of and tacitly approved of the sinful relationship. Most likely, however, there were those in the church who saw the danger of the violation but didn't know what to do about it. It is possible that a portion of the Corinthians were overstepping the newfound freedom from the old law, but due to a lack of spiritual maturity they did not make proper spiritual decisions. Blomberg cites the vagaries of newly formed *enlightenment*: "The church's reaction to this affair was as bad or worse than the affair itself. Instead of grieving over sin in their midst, they were actually smug over their newfound 'enlightened' tolerance as Christians (v.2)" (104-105).

Paul's Response

Despite being hundreds of miles removed from the Corinthian church, Paul projects himself into the ugly situation with critique and instruction. He forthrightly condemns the pride of those who tolerated the sinful relationship, suggesting that some were even celebrating the presence of sin. In the place of prideful boasting he suggests grieving and goes so far as to lead them literally to excommunicate the sinful man. Paul's instruction is threefold: First, take the violation seriously. Second, grieve over the moral laxness seemingly present in each person in the church. Third, throw the bum out!

This is an ingenious plan for the "teachable moment" confronting the church. They had yet to see gross sin as an affront to God and as an impediment to God's presence within the fellowship. There was a need for them to see the ugly reality of the sin they tolerated. The focus was clearly on the good of the whole church and not on the needs of a single person. If the church was to make it out of the first century intact, hard decisions needed to be made.

Throw the Bum Out!

It seems a bit out of New Testament character to remove someone officially from a church fellowship. In fact, this is the only example of full excommunication in the New Testament. Paul justifies the removal of the sinful man on the basis of the Hebrew Passover practice of disposing of the old leaven before the sacrifice was undertaken. The Passover reference would no doubt be foreign to many in the Gentile-heavy Corinthian fellowship. However, the metaphorical significance of his statements would not be lost on the Corinthians. They were told what to do and why they should do so. Paul seemed confident they would assemble and do the right thing.

What Happened to the Man?

The question of what happened to the sinful man has been debated for centuries. Did he clean up his act and return? Did bitterness overtake him and turn him away from the church forever? Did Satan "get him"? No one knows the final disposition of the man. He is not mentioned again by Paul or any other New Testament writer. No doubt he was expelled from the church with the hope that he would recognize the need for genuine repentance, experience such, and return to the fellowship.

The more relevant question is "What happened to the church?" We know the answer to that question. The First Church of Dysfunction, a.k.a. the Corinthian Church, heeded the instruction of Paul and grew into one of the strongest churches of the second century. Possibly the first major step in that direction came with the decision to excommunicate the sinful man. As harsh as that move had to have been, it was necessary for the future of the church. Again, Paul was placing the needs of the larger body over the needs of a single person.

Final Instructions

After dealing with the unique sin and the subsequent removal of the individual, Paul provides a blanket instruction as to tolerating sin within a fellowship. He makes the case that it is unhealthy for a church to allow overt, unrepentant, and obvious sinners to be associated with it. If a person claims to be in Christ yet is identifiable as a greedy, idolatrous, slanderous, prone to drunkenness, a cheat or sexually immoral, he or she must be disassociated from those seeking to live righteously. Paul even states that a person who embodies any of the above negatives shouldn't be aligned with, most likely due to the possibility of contamination. Since a great portion of their church activities included community meals, this was a serious statement. Paul's instructions however, apply only to Christians who exhibit obvious sin in their lives. Believers are to continue to interact with those outside of Christ for the purpose of influencing and reaching them with the grace of salvation. These teachings must not be taken out of context and become an impediment to outreach and evangelism.

Life Lessons

It is important to focus on the consistent messages of this section. This is less a primer on excommunication than instruction on the necessity for purity in thought and action among a body of believers. Overt serial sin will be a drain on the entire fellowship of Christians within a church. All people in the church will be affected in ways both minor and major. This type of sin will become an impediment for God's progressive movement. The church must be on guard to protect the overall body from the true ravages of runaway sin. Since today's church doesn't have a literal Paul to act as its "conscience in action," the mantle falls elsewhere. However, we continue to have a "virtual Paul" through his New Testament letters. No excuse exists today, just as no excuse existed in first-century Corinth.

One Bad Apple

1. Describe ways in which the relationship between the man and his stepmother was sinful.

_____

_____

_____

_____

_____

_____

2. In your view, why did Paul not major on the sexual sin present in the Corinthian church?

_____

_____

_____

_____

_____

_____

3. Paul's view held that a single person's sin could damage the entire fellowship. Identify ways in which this could occur.

_____

_____

_____

_____

_____

_____

4. How were members of the church guilty of sin in relation to the illicit sexual relationship occurring within the fellowship?

_____

_____

_____

_____

5. Identify reasons you either agree or disagree with Paul's instructions to remove the man from the church.

_____
_____
_____
_____
_____
_____

6. Why was the stepmother not mentioned again by Paul?

_____
_____
_____
_____
_____
_____

7. What theological significance is to be found here?

_____
_____
_____
_____
_____
_____

8. Should today's church utilize these teachings of Paul and remove people from the church due to obvious sin? Explain the possible ramifications of your response.

_____
_____
_____
_____
_____
_____

One Bad Apple

9. How do these teachings impact the relationships between Christians and non-Christians?

_____

_____

_____

_____

_____

_____

The State of Unions

1 Corinthians 7

The issue of marriage obviously loomed large in the Corinthian church. Questions and issues were provided to Paul for his counsel and instruction. The questions must have covered the entire scope of marriage since Paul provided commentary on so many facets.

In total, Paul presents a moderate philosophy on Christian marriage. He certainly doesn't come across as being "anti-female," which is a routine accusation against him. He does however declare that when all things are considered, the Corinthians would be better off remaining single. His reasoning is purely spiritual and Kingdom-oriented. Paul solidly believed that the return of Christ would occur during this lifetime (or within the lives of the generation to which he ministered). With this operational belief in place, marriage could provide an impediment to ministry. To be unfettered by familial responsibility would be a unique freedom to *live* ministry.

Paul was a pragmatist, however, and knew his readers were interested in combining marriage together with their new faith. Thus, he provides instruction that is both thorough and complete.

Good Not to Marry, but . . .

As mentioned above, Paul was bold in his belief that it is a better life-state to be single. Again, he is not being anti-female, nor anti-marriage in vv. 1-2. He simply demonstrates his focus on doing God's work with a unique totality of commitment. When Paul states, "It is good for a man not to marry," "good" is best defined as expedient or profitable. Again, he refers to the world situation for a first century believer. Due to rampant persecution and all that was at stake with the progress of the new church, it was simply best not to be encumbered by a spouse.

This whole chapter is dominated by the expectation of the imminent Parousia. Responsibility toward children and the generations to come does not enter into the apostle's calculations, for he thought of himself as living not in the first century but in the last. Marriage was of doubtful wisdom because it might divert from individual attention to the work of the Lord (Craig, 76).

However, Paul recognized that not all believers would be as serious as he was about life and faith. This is actually a massive understatement since chances are no one else shared his level of commitment. To clarify the point, he cites rampant immorality as a cause for the need for marriage. Is Paul being wishy-washy? I don't think so. Reality is the reason Paul cites both the optimum state of union and the likely necessity for Christians to marry. We must not forget that Corinth was the church that seemingly boasted the illicit relationship between a stepson and his stepmother. Immorality was an issue both within and outside the church. Marriage, in effect, would create a barrier against this type of insidious sin. Plus, sexual relations of various types were staples of many pagan religions that existed in cosmopolitan communities like Corinth. The need to create a truly Christian view of sexuality was paramount.

Fulfilling the Marital Duty

While some no doubt wish Paul had included marital issues such as picking up clutter and washing dishes, he focused on basic sexual relations between husband and wife in vv. 3-5. As always, a pressing need preceded such instruction, and in this case it was the mistaken view that sexual abstinence would lead to heightened spirituality. Due to the influence of Stoic and Essene philosophy, sexual intercourse came to be seen as debasing the inner spiritual self. Paul, both single and celibate, was instructing that celibacy had no place in the Christian marriage. In effect, husband and wife own each other in a unique way that merges the physical with the spiritual. Any deprivation of sexual intimacy must be of mutual consent and should be for only short periods of time. Plus, the agreed upon time should be dedicated to spiritual devotion and development.

Paul ends the paragraph with a major reason as to why he places such importance on sexual relations in marriage. Any prolonged period of celibacy between husband and wife could open the door to all forms of temptation and subsequent sins. It is important to remember that Corinth was uniquely worldly and most sexual sins were openly embraced.

To Singles and Widows

Once again Paul offers his deeply felt belief that the most productive state for Christians in Corinth was singleness. He specifically cites those who have never married and surviving spouses as being truly single. To these he encourages the status quo, but if lust and other sexual desires were problematic, then they should marry.

To ones who were married but now are widows, it is a good thing to be like Paul because this gives greater opportunity to work for Christ. On the other hand, he recognizes that few have the gift of self-control to refrain from sexual relationships. The "good" of celibacy must be balanced with the teaching of Genesis 2:18, where God said it was "not good" for man to be alone. "It is better to marry than to burn": Those who burn with passion should go ahead and marry rather than struggle with sexual passion (Romacher & House, 45).

There is no doubting the fact that Paul viewed the optimum life-state of a Christian as being single. Again, he is not oddly anti-marriage, but simply prone to believe that all believers should be as fervent and committed as he is. He obviously sees special opportunity in the single state to serve God better. However, rather than command singleness, he opts for the union of marriage in an effort to eradicate the issue of illicit passions.

Thou Shalt Not Divorce

Scripture is remarkably consistent when it comes to divorce in Christian marriages. Jesus cited divorce as being completely against God's purposes, and Paul echoes his statements. Matthew was the only New Testament writer who added the adultery stipulation, which allowed for divorce if adultery was involved. Paul directly applies the teachings of Jesus to the question of divorce among believers in Corinth.

It is clear that Jesus wanted to stop the many frivolous reasons for divorce that had become the norm in Hebrew life. Fee writes, "Although his concern was with the 'why' of divorce within his own culture (to be rid of a wife in order to have another), by placing marriage back within the creational mandate of Genesis 2:24, Jesus in effect interpreted the seventh commandment to mean no divorce" (293).

Paul also addressed the intricacies of melding the Hebrew tradition of the wife having no divorce options with the Greco-Roman equality of freedom shared by both sexes. Oddly, Paul actually addresses the female in these verses: "a wife must not separate from her husband." Most likely this was to acknowledge that with the newly found freedom of Christianity comes new responsibilities for both males and females.

The bottom line is simply this: The Corinthians were instructed not to divorce. If divorce had already taken place, they were told to remain single or to be reconciled to the former spouse. Remarriage for believers was certainly not an option.

Paul is providing a new (or renewed) framework for the Christian life, one in which marriage is linked to the spiritual union of believers and the church. Marriage was to be seen as holy and as an exercise in commitment, one modeled after the relationship of Christ and the church.

What about "mixed marriages," those between *unequally yoked* Christians and non-Christians? Paul goes on to stipulate that if a man or woman is married to a non-Christian, they should remain married. Obviously there were those in Corinth who jettisoned their "unequally yoked" spouse due to their new faith in Christ. Paul saw this decision as an actual affront to faith in Christ. So he urges those in mixed marriage to remain married in order to lead their spouse to faith in Christ. However, Paul recognized the unique situation for both the believer and non-believers and allows for the unbelieving spouse to leave in peace, if they so choose.

The consistent New Testament teaching on divorce has been much maligned and even abused in the modern church. It must not be overlooked, however, that both Jesus and Paul had the universal church in mind when speaking on the dark issue of divorce. Even though Paul addressed a dysfunctional group and Jesus attempted to "Christianize marriage" and stem the flow of frivolous divorces, their teachings do create the overall New Testament approach to divorce.

Guiding Principal: Stay as You Are

Paul's consistent theme throughout chapter 7 is that we simply remain in the life station we presently have and pursue God from there. If we are single, then we should remain single with our first and foremost focus being on serving God. If we are married, then we should remain married and together focus on serving God. Paul added additional stipulations and qualifications, but the overall theme is clear and, for Paul, quite flexible.

Life Lessons

While it is tempting to view Paul's teachings on singleness, marriage, and divorce as being archaically first century, it would be wrong to do so. Paul's statements on the life-state of Christians are foundational to all New Testament doctrine and belief. Even today his teachings must be recognized as orthodox and genuine and should form the framework of how we live. There's also a great deal to be learned from his idea that life's number one priority should be service to the Kingdom of God. The temptation is great in today's social climate to prioritize personal achievement, personal pleasure, the pursuit of happiness, and the importance of family over service to God. The prevalent opinion that "God is an afterthought" does not separate today's world from that of the first century as much as we might think.

The following are possibly the greatest lessons to be learned from 1 Corinthians 7:

- Whether married or single, place primary focus on serving God.
- Sexual temptation will always be an impediment to full devotion and should be resisted by all Christians.
- Divorce is not part of God's great design.
- In marriages between Christians and non-Christians, the believing spouse should live in positive ways in order to lead the nonbelieving spouse to faith in Christ.
- Live with the intense expectancy of the return of Christ.

1. Identify possible reasons for Paul's reputation as being "anti-female."

_____

_____

_____

_____

_____

_____

2. Why did Paul believe it was better for a Christian to remain single?

_____

_____

_____

_____

_____

_____

3. What cultural, social, and Greek religious factors were prevalent in Corinth that could lead to sin on the part of single believers?

_____

_____

_____

_____

_____

_____

4. Briefly describe the marital duty views of Paul.

_____

_____

_____

_____

_____

_____

5. What advice does Paul provide for widows?

_____

_____

_____

_____

_____

_____

6. What cultural or religious factors influence Paul's teaching on divorce?

_____

_____

_____

_____

_____

_____

7. Describe Paul's views on a "mixed marriage."

_____

_____

_____

_____

_____

_____

8. How did the idea that Christ's return was imminent affect all of Paul's teaching on relationships?

_____

_____

_____

_____

_____

_____

Carnivorous Corinthians

Paul uses this chapter to formulate a response to questions raised by the Corinthians concerning eating meat that had been sacrificed to a pagan deity or idol. This seemly innocuous issue became disconcerting in the new fellowship and quickly moved toward becoming destructive in ways both major and minor.

Much like the Hebrews, the various pagan temples offered sacrifices of quality living animals in their practice of worship. The surplus meat was sold in meat markets across Corinth, so the possibility of purchasing meat that had entertained pagans in temple rituals was all but absolute. This reality gave pause to many new Christians who reasoned that such meat would be spiritually contaminated in some way. Taken a step further, would eating meat sacrificed to a pagan god be vicarious idol worship and an affront to Christ? Additionally, those who had converted from Judaism had been instructed that such meat would render them spiritually unclean and was thus against the Mosaic Law. It is easy to see how this issue became such a genuine dilemma for many new believers in the church.

Problem 1: Knowledge

Being Greco-Roman, reason, logic, and acquired knowledge were prized in Corinth. Unfortunately, this mind-set went against the grain of Christian teaching. New Testament writers share the view that there is a difference between basic knowledge and Christian wisdom. The New Testament also affirms that knowledge alone is not sufficient for Christian growth or as a basis for Christian behavior. Fee writes:

> The problem is primarily attitudinal. They think Christian conduct is predicated on knowledge and that knowledge gives them rights and freedom to act as they will in this matter. Paul has another view: The content of their knowledge is only partially correct; but more importantly, knowledge is not the grounding of Christian behavior, love is. (363)

A primary issue concerning knowledge in this case was the gross inequity in existence within the church. Making up the Corinthian church were former Hebrews and Gentiles from an amazing variety of backgrounds. Levels of faith and maturity were held in varying degrees among the fellowship of believers in Corinth. Most likely, the percentage of mature believers was quite small in this church, as it would have been in all early churches. It is apparent that the "stronger" believers were condescending to the "weaker" believers and the result was church turmoil and theological problems. To the knowledgeable, mature group, there was nothing wrong with eating sacrificial meat. To the less knowledgeable, less mature group, there were many wrongs associated with the sacrificial meat quandary. To this group, it was a prime spiritual issue. To the mature group, this issue was all but laughable. One can see how pernicious this seemingly innocuous item had become.

By the cultural definitions of the day, knowledge itself would never be seen as a problem. Only in the counter-culture, counter-reason dimension of faith is the difference made manifest. Historically, culture has prized the accumulation of knowledge. Francis Bacon is famous for the line "Knowledge is power." There is no doubt that he is right in the truest cultural sense. Knowledge brings both power and personal advantage. However, the New Testament is clear that love (agape) is foundational to faith, never knowledge.

In v. 2 Paul writes, "Anyone who claims to know something does not yet have the necessary knowledge." Ellingworth and Hatton paraphrase v. 2 in this manner: "If a person thinks that he has attained some degree of knowledge, he has not yet reached the state where he has any knowledge at all in the real sense of the word" (160).

Problem 2: Love

Verse 3 summarizes the problems surrounding knowledge in Corinth: "But anyone who loves God is known by God." The answer to the dilemma is clear; knowledge must be subordinate to love if it is to be genuine. Put another way, the key to faith and faith living is to place love (agape) as the predicate to Christian knowledge. To know God personally is both to love God and to be loved by God. One of the principal fruits that grow from this reciprocal love is genuine Christian knowledge.

Clement of Egypt cites Paul's words in v. 2 in this way:

> If anyone thinks he has arrived at knowledge,
> he does not yet know as he ought to know;
> but
> If anyone loves,
> this one truly knows. (Fee, 367)

In his classic chapter on love (1 Cor 13). Paul always places love above knowledge. Agape love as the predicate for knowledge becomes the application of knowledge. This can be seen most clearly by contrasting the two approaches to knowledge. In purely human ways, knowledge extends the individual and provides for advantage. In terms of faith, knowledge is limited by love, thus allowing for the needs of others to take precedence—which is, by the way, the practical definition of agape love.

Mature believers in Corinth maximized advantage over the less mature due to their superior knowledge. It is as if they flaunted their superiority at the expense of the newer believers. Again, advantage gained by the misapplication of knowledge results in dysfunction within the church.

The key balance in Corinth would have been a proper understanding of the limits of knowledge in contrast to supernatural wisdom. In faith, knowledge is to be led by love in both understanding and application. This combination accomplishes an environment for both mature believers and newer Christians to thrive in unison.

Problem 3: Stumbling Blocks

For the seasoned Corinthian believer, the notion of tainted meat due to pagan ritual was somewhat absurd. That said, Paul obviously didn't see this as the real issue in play within the Corinthian fellowship. With one simple sentence, he leaped over the self-reported problem to the real issue of knowledge becoming a stumbling block for the less mature believers.

Blomberg likens this to a "rights" issue with v. 9 providing the thesis statement for the paragraph: "*Stumbling block* and that which *causes one to fall into sin* (v. 13) are synonyms and help explain each other. The 'exercise of your freedom' reads more literally *your authority* or *your right*. In short, v. 9 urges Christians not to demand their rights that cause fellow Christians to sin" (162-63).

Paul effectively states that if eating meat in Corinth becomes a stumbling block for less mature Christians, he would give up the eating of meat. Paul voluntarily gives up his "right" to eat meat. He abdicates his knowledge and demonstrates love by also abstaining from meat. This exhibition of love would both honor and protect the younger believers.

Anything to the contrary would be flawed Christian reasoning and clearly against his teaching. The focus on wisdom is to be spiritual in nature, with spirituality allowing for the needs of others to be considered first. In so doing, a mature believer would abstain from eating sacrificial food in the interest of weaker believers. If not, the possibility for becoming a stumbling block would exist. It shouldn't be lost on anyone that when a new Christian sees non-Christian behavior in professed believers, it *is* non-Christian behavior. Perception defines reality, at least until the point of positive growth and spiritual maturity. Until that point is reached, the nod should be given to the less mature of the faith.

Life Lessons

It is apparent that the modern church does not face issues related to idol sacrifice. Trying to make a direct application is impossible and, truthfully, fruitless. The real beauty in Paul's response to this issue does, however, hold universal application. We are to be aware of our responsibilities to both non-Christians and newer Christians so as not become a stumbling block to them. A mature Christian knows that cutting the grass on Sunday is not a sinful act. However, if it is perceived as such by someone else and the possibility of becoming a stumbling block exists, it could become a problematic practice. In cases such as this, perception does define reality and we become responsible for both the lost and the less mature Christian.

We should also be aware that knowledge is always to be subordinate to love. Love is to be the rule in all activities, relationships, and practices. Knowledge is a wonderful thing, but it is spiritual only when it accompanies love.

1. Describe how meat became an issue in the Corinthian fellowship.

_____

_____

_____

_____

_____

_____

2. How could knowledge "puff up" as James writes and become the impediment it became in Corinth?

_____

_____

_____

_____

_____

_____

3. Describe the likely reasons Hebrew believers had for thinking of Gentile Christians as inferior.

_____

_____

_____

_____

_____

_____

4. Describe ways in which people tend to subordinate love to knowledge.

_____

_____

_____

_____

_____

_____

5. Describe Paul's preference of always subordinating knowledge to love.

_____

_____

_____

_____

_____

_____

6. List ways the more mature Christians in Corinth had become stumbling blocks to the newer, less mature believers.

_____

_____

_____

_____

_____

_____

7. Describe modern examples of the "meat sacrificed to idols" issue faced by the Christians.

_____

_____

_____

_____

_____

_____

8. In the face of modern examples, describe how the full application of agape love would possibly negate the problems.

_____

_____

_____

_____

_____

_____

Misbehaving in Church

1 Corinthians 11

In this section, Paul deals with issues relating to actions and practices during worship and times of fellowship in the Christian church. Once again, the Corinthians exhibited flair in their forms of dysfunction. It seems they couldn't be satisfied with ordinary problems; they once more raised the bar and gave Paul opportunity for correction.

There are two unlinked and contrasting issues in play in this chapter. The first is a uniquely confusing treatise on head coverings aimed at both males and females in the church. The second has to do with actions and attitudes related to the sacramental practice of communion. Each problem area did find a common link in a basic irreverence exhibited toward corporate worship and fellowship.

Head Issues

It is good to state up front that it is impossible to ascertain the full meaning of these confusing and somewhat disjointed sections. While opinions are plentiful, no one really knows exactly what Paul was teaching. Some see the issue as relating to veils worn by women, while others think it had more to do with hairstyles. Relating to males, it is assumed by some that Paul condemned long hair. Others believe that the men of the church had begun wearing Hebrew prayer shawls and went to the extent of draping them across their heads. Of course, there are those who see it all as entirely metaphorical and symptomatic of unnamed issues understood only by the first century Corinthians.

In all probability, Paul may have referred both to veils on women and hairstyles of men and women. While seemingly insignificant, these issues could rupture the peace of a multiethnic church. Hebrew women traditionally were expected to wear veils to religious activities, while Gentile Greek women didn't follow similar practices. Also, due to the numerous pagan temples and overall cosmopolitan makeup of Corinth, many styles of dress and hair were common. Long, unkempt hair on both men and women was associated with people of loose morals, while very short hair on women would be seen as resembling the masculine partner in a homosexual relationship or a convicted adulteress. It is possible Paul simply instructed the Corinthians to be as reverent with their appearance as they were with their hearts.

No doubt the earlier teaching on freedom would apply here. Even though a Corinthian Christian is free to dress and groom as much as they wish, responsibility accompanies this freedom. If the exercise of personal freedom causes damage to the church or becomes a stumbling block for others, freedom is to give way to love.

This truth could easily apply to dress, hairstyle, or both. Common conformity combined with reverence and love could be Paul's main goal in this difficult section.

Head as a Metaphor

Those who see Paul as harboring an anti-female bias point to his seeming subordination of women in vv. 3-10. While these verses are almost as peculiar as those dealing with head coverings, there is a distinguished flow within them. While Paul may purposely subordinate women to men here, most likely he is reminding all believers of the origin of both men and women. Gnostic beliefs of the day sought to blend the sexes into a "pristine androgynous ideal" (Blomberg, 214). The New Testament is both consistent and clear in not blurring the line between the sexes. Neither does it teach that sexual differences and roles were not by design.

There are several options for dealing with these verses. Possibly the most wholesome option for today's church is to see Paul as citing the creative order followed by functionality. Temptation exists to cite this section as an absolute teaching of man's hierarchical status above women. Many yield to that temptation and thus take the easy road toward restricting women from ministry by citing their lack of authority. The foremost reason this is a mistake is simply that Paul did not object to the praying and prophesying of women in the church. It is a known fact that women took part in both worship leadership and teaching in this church. Did Paul miss that fact and thus miss an opportunity to further bash women? Not likely; Paul was so astute that he would be the person who could find the proverbial needle in the haystack. This is not about women's status or participation in ministry; it is about source and function.

Again, no one knows the real issue that preceded Paul's response. One can only speculate that the females' newly found freedom and equal status had caused some to go to extremes. Possibly some females wanted to "one-up" men and usurp even more freedom. Or were women dressing in such ways that their "roles" were being blurred? Despite the absence of a reason, we can sense the important elements and infer certain truths. God is the ultimate source of all people and of genuine faith. God created an order replete with roles and function for both men and women. If life is lived contrary to these basics, life will merge away from God's intended paths. Paul saw this condition as an impediment to worship.

Agape Feast and Communion

Leave it to the dysfunctional Corinthians to find ways to ruin a feast named after selfless love. Verse 17b literally reads, "For you come together not for the better but for the worse." The church came together for a common meal and during the meal they would experience communion. Furnish reports that "their ritual sharing of bread and cup took place in connection with an ordinary meal consisting of food brought along by the participants themselves. It appears that there were two separate ritual actions, the sharing of the common loaf likely occurring before the meal, and the sharing of a common cup at its conclusion" (79).

Paul reacted to certain actions and practices that occurred during these quasi-communal gatherings. The abuses were out of line with an agape feast, and some were spiritually out of line as well. Fee sees the abuses moving in two directions, "horizontal and vertical" (532).

Horizontal Issues

Cliques had formed within the church and were in evidence during the meal. Paul cites practices of some beginning to eat before all had arrived; some were left out and went hungry while some actually got drunk. It is obvious that Paul didn't feel communion and fellowship among this crowd.

Vertical Issues

It is clear from the interpersonal abuses that there would also be spiritual problems. Paul tells the Corinthians that participation in the symbolic Lord's Supper is to be regarded as highly sacred. Their frivolous approach to including it into a not-so-common meal rife with class distinctions was a serious abuse of the sacrifice of Christ. "Do this in remembrance of me" runs to the heart of what communion is to be and thus sets a standard. Fee puts it this way:

> The bread represents his crucified body, which, along with his poured out blood, effected the death that ratified the New Covenant. By their abuse of one another, they were also abusing the one through whose death and resurrection they had been brought to life and formed into this new fellowship. *Do this*, these words remind them, *in remembrance of me*. To which Paul adds, "for as often as we celebrate this meal we proclaim the Lord's death until he comes." Believers eat in the present in fellowship with one another, focusing on Christ's death which brought them life; and they do so as eschatological people, awaiting his return. (533)

Communion is an act of the present that celebrates the past while holding a passionate hope for the future, all focused on Christ. The Corinthians completely missed this purpose.

Life Lessons

Not every element of Paul's response to worship behavior has direct, modern application. The final section focusing on the sacredness of the Lord's Supper has the most universal appeal. While we do not tack communion onto a raucous meal rife with inequality and poor taste, we do tend to tack it onto an otherwise routine worship service.

Then there's the habit of celebrating this sacrament only on the fifth Sunday of the odd month. Is that practice found in the book of Numbers? Paul's main instruction is for each participant to take communion seriously, even to the level of the sacred. That alone could change lives and churches.

As to the earlier portions of Corinthians 11, it is all but impossible to make precise application of the teaching pertaining to the "head" issues. Possibly the best we can do is to see that our origin and source is God and that we each have roles and functions to provide for the Kingdom. Take heart, however, for Paul was not being restrictive in this teaching. These are words of freedom and purpose to be experienced within God's order. Rather than being restrictive and confining, they are more genuinely reflective of God's marvelous plan of equality. When combined with Galatians 3:25-28, they speak of inclusion built on joint faith in Christ.

> But now you have arrived at your destination: By faith in Christ you are in direct relationship with God. Your baptism in Christ was not just washing you up for a fresh start. It also involved dressing you in an adult faith wardrobe—Christ's life, the fulfillment of God's original purpose. In Christ's family there can be no division into Jew or non-Jew, slave and free, male and female. Among us you are all equal. That is, we are all in a common relationship with Jesus Christ. (Eugene Peterson, *The Message*)

1. Describe reasons why dress and hairstyle were potentially problematic in Corinth.

_____

_____

_____

_____

_____

_____

2. How do the issues of freedom and responsibility factor into this section?

_____

_____

_____

_____

_____

_____

3. List your feelings regarding Paul's views and treatment of females in this section.

_____

_____

_____

_____

_____

_____

4. Describe the possible implications of the created order of the sexes in contrast to roles and functions.

_____

_____

_____

_____

_____

5. Determine and describe how females in the church were overreacting or overreaching in their participation.

_____

_____

_____

_____

_____

6. Describe ways in which the Corinthians were abusing the communion feasts.

_____

_____

_____

_____

_____

_____

7. List ways in which following Christ's words of "do this in remembrance of me" could alter the purpose and participation of the Lord's Supper.

_____

_____

_____

_____

_____

_____

8. In the Corinthian church, the odd but divisive issues were dress and hairstyle. What would today's issues be?

_____

_____

_____

_____

_____

6   The Way Most Excellent

1 Corinthians 13

Chapter 13 is Paul's New Testament opus. It is easily the best known of all his writings. It is recited at weddings and other special occasions. It is poetic and flowing, filled with "parallels and symmetry" (Watson, 140). But what does it really mean? What was Paul's aim in waxing so poetically in an otherwise harsh response to a dysfunctional lot?

It is best to see these famous words as a continuation of his corrective teaching on spiritual gifts in chapter 12. The Corinthians had been abusing spiritual gifts in both concept and practice. This, combined with the dearth of genuine selflessness in play among the Corinthian Christians, provided Paul with the need to flesh out "agape" love fully.

One must not forget that this is the church Paul earlier accused of abiding sin that even pagans wouldn't tolerate. This is the church that split into factions over preferred church leaders and trivialized worship and communion. Now they were abusing spiritual gifts by again valuing knowledge over love.

Chapter 13 is a flowing definition of genuine Christian love and simultaneously a statement on the intended structure of spiritual gifts. "While spiritual gifts are important to the functioning of the body (church), they lose their value if love is not behind them. Love is more important than all the spiritual gifts existing in the Christian body; love is the 'way most excellent' (12:31 NIV) for believers to use their gifts" (Osborne, 186).

The best method for understanding Paul's message in this section is to do as he did and view each statement as distinct. Again, it shouldn't be lost on today's reader that Paul portrayed the central necessity of love while at the same time pointing out the faults of the Corinthians. All in all, that is not a bad way to utilize these verses today.

13:1—*If I speak in the tongues of mortals and of angels, but do not have love, I am only a noisy gong or a clanging cymbal.* Tongues-speak was a routine practice in the Greek-pagan religions of Corinth. As these practices meshed with new Christian ones, several possible abuses came to light. Pride and being "puffed up" also dampened the fellowship as tongues-speak led to feelings of spiritual superiority. So even if a person could speak in "all languages, human or divine" (Hodge, 235), but did so without selfless love as the basis, their gift would be void. In essence, it is not the ability but the motivation that's important.

13:2—*And if I have prophetic powers, and understand all mysteries and all knowledge, and if I have all faith, so as to remove mountains, but do not have love, I am nothing.* Hodge describes this as a literal grab for total and complete knowledge and power, ". . . that I may know all mysteries and have all knowledge that I may have all faith" (237). This *cornering the market* state of full faith giftedness should allow for the greatest spirituality, but Paul again cites it as worthless without love as its base. Once again, knowledge regardless of degree must be subordinate to love.

13:3—*If I give all I possess to the poor and surrender my body to the flames, but have not love, I gain nothing.* Paul moves to actual practice at this point, saying that even martyrdom is wasted if done for reasons other than love. One could give away inheritance and fortune, as did Francis of Assisi, or provide for great self-sacrifice, but do so for the wrong reasons. Paul places zero value on sacrifice, even to the point of death, if the sacrifice is done for any reason save love.

13:4—*Love is patient.* Paul adds virtues as attributes of love as the basis for life. Patience can be seen as having a "long mind" and not being shaken by negative events. Another approach would be the traditional view of patience as "long suffering" combined with a a view of the future based on God's ultimate victory. This could easily define John's intent in Revelation as he sought patience from the heavily-persecuted late first century church.

Love is kind. The Greek word translated as "kind" is used only here in the New Testament. It is akin to the other focused definition of "agape." It is also a word that is not intent on reciprocity. One is to be kind out of love, regardless of a response in return.

Love is not envious . . . To remove envy as a possibility, one must first remove self-centeredness. To put others first is not to get hung up on what others have or what they do. To conquer envy is also to triumph over hatred, rivalry, greed, and feelings of self-entitlement.

. . . or boastful . . . All gifts should be used without the need for or expectation of the spotlight. Gifts are to be exercised for the Kingdom of God and not for the personal edification of the believer.

. . . or arrogant . . . Conceit is a good word to substitute here and is a precedent to further negatives, such as boasting, envy, and self-entitlement.

13:5— *. . . or rude.* Wholesome would work here, as would decorous. Mare defines rude as "behaving disgracefully" and believes Paul was obliquely referring to the disorderly manner Corinthians employed while in worship and the communion meal (268).

It does not insist on its own way. Once again, love is contrasted against the human tendencies of self-absorption and focusing on one's own needs. Gifts are to be employed in a spirit of selflessness for others, never for the elevation of the individual.

It is not irritable or resentful. In this case, Paul is promoting love over knowledge. One is to endure slights, insults, and affronts by acknowledging that love is the most excellent choice. If the slights are internalized and viewed through the lens of humanity, provocations and response will surely follow. If that option is followed, love will be nowhere in sight.

13:6—*It does not rejoice in wrongdoing, but rejoices in the truth.* If you've ever taken pleasure from the trials of another person, you have "rejoiced in wrongdoing." To rejoice in the truth is to hold to God's standard in all things. This verse is also held to mean that believers should not view unrighteousness with favor; quite the opposite is true.

13:7—*It bears all things* . . . "Bears all things" could mean that because of love a Christian can put up with anything and remain committed. Some view this statement as meaning that the faults of others are to be disposed of and no record is to be kept of wrongs. Another view is that genuine love will protect relationships by not allowing for a list of wrongs to be called up and used over and over.

Seen in light of God's grace, it could be that while wrongs cannot be actually forgotten, there is the assurance that they will not be used against us in the future.

. . . believes all things . . . This trust could be supernatural, in that love provides for ultimate trusting (faith), or that it always seeks the best in others.

. . . hopes all things . . . Again, this could be a supernatural, eternal hope, or simply wishing the best for others in all ways.

. . .endures all things. The Greek word is a military term and means to sustain the assault of an enemy. Persecution and hardship were in ready evidence in the first century church, and Paul was declaring that love would sustain them and provide stamina.

13:8-10—*Love never ends. But as for prophecies, they will come to an end; as for tongues, they will cease; as for knowledge, it will come to an end. For we know only in part and we prophesy only in part; but when the complete comes, the partial will come to an end.* Agape love is not a temporal, emotion feeling but a life-state. The gifts in play that are to be fueled by love are indeed temporary. "Spiritual gifts will end because they are given to build God's Kingdom" (Osborn, 191). The need for gifts will come to an end, but the foundational love that propelled genuine giftedness will carry forward into eternal life.

13:11-12—These verses build upon the precious ones in contrasting the capacity for full spiritual understanding in this life with the "perfect" existence of eternity. One can know and do only so much in this life in comparison to the life to follow.

13:13—*And now faith, hope and love abide, these three; and the greatest of these is love.* There are two distinct schools of thought on this verse. First, Paul broke with practice and tradition by not citing these three attributes as being equal. This is unprecedented and thus requires interpretation. It is possible that believers will require neither faith nor hope in the age to come, leaving love as the only permanent gift.

The other view is that faith, hope, and love are the fruit of the Spirit and shouldn't be confused with gifts of the Spirit. Gifts will cease but the fruit of the Spirit will transcend this existence into the one to follow.

Conclusion: Paul's 1 Corinthians 13 was, as always, a means to an end. Gifts were being abused in various ways and were the cause of additional dysfunction. The tendency toward being selfish rather than selfless was rampant among the Corinthian Christians. Paul's writings placed heavy emphasis on the inner realities of faith and cited the utter uselessness of faith practice built on anything other than love. Stopping short of stating "It's about love, stupid," Paul in essence makes that claim by dismantling the self-serving mind-set of superior gifts and consequent divisions apparent in the Corinthian church.

Life Lessons

It is a sad but true reality that many people see 1 Corinthians 13 as nothing more than a stand-alone chapter of poetic writing focusing on love. These words have been read at countless weddings, funerals, and ceremonies in attempts to promote the supremacy of love. Was this Paul's overriding intent as he wrote this now infamous text? It is probably safe to say no; Paul did indeed have other issues in mind as he made the transition from chapter 12 to chapter 13.

It is apparent from a complete study of the First Letter that Chapters 12 and 13 are inseparable. To fully comprehend the more famous chapter 13 and honor its contextual integrity, it is necessary to include the negatives of the previous chapter into the beautiful lyrics of love in chapter 13.

When this is accomplished, the true beauty of chapter 13 shines forth. Paul is teaching all who read with completeness that love is the key to both spiritual gifts and supernatural wisdom. Taken a step further, Paul is actually teaching that love is to be the sum total of all faith exercises and activities. Spiritual gifts of all levels must be exercised out of love for God and other people. Spiritual gifts are to be discerned through genuine spiritual wisdom. Love is to be the common denominator in all such activities, regardless of the stature or flair of individual gifts.

Chances are that no one who reads these words will be burned as a martyr or give away all earthly possessions to aid the poor. The best we can hope for is to honor God by effectively exercising spiritual gifts out of genuine wisdom and love. Most likely this was Paul's basic hope for the Corinthians as well, for one doesn't have to be a martyr to learn to love!

1. Describe how and why knowledge must be subordinate to love.

_____

_____

_____

_____

_____

_____

2. Identify ways that love can cover the faults of others rather than delighting in them.

_____

_____

_____

_____

_____

_____

3. Contrast agape love with other forms and types of love.

_____

_____

_____

_____

_____

_____

4. Identify reasons that both faith and hope are supernatural traits when associated with agape love.

_____

_____

_____

_____

_____

_____

5. As associated with prophesies and knowledge, describe how love is permanent.

_____

_____

_____

_____

_____

_____

6. Identify ways in which a believer could still be reasoning and thinking as a child does (13:11).

_____

_____

_____

_____

_____

_____

7. How does love affect the process of one day knowing in full? (13:12)

_____

_____

_____

_____

_____

_____

8. How and why is love the greatest among the three that remain? (13:13)

_____

_____

_____

_____

_____

7 The New, New Covenant

The art of salesmanship was alive and well in first century Corinth. Long before the invention of the resume and vita, there existed a practice of credentialing known as *letters of recommendation.* In order for an itinerant preacher, teacher, or philosopher to gain wide acceptance and thus, an audience, statements of prior performance and basic authenticity were needed. At this unique point in time, the practice of roving communicators from various disciplines was prevalent. In order to make a living, these speakers were forced to move around from place to place, effectively starting over in each new locale. To be granted any type of audience, it was necessary for them to provide letters of reference that would validate their qualifications or at least say enough nice things about them so they could "try out" for the needed audience. As Belleville states, "Much like today Paul lived in a mobile society that placed similar value on personal achievements and introductory letters. Itinerant speakers, in particular, were expected to carry letters of reference with them as they traveled from place to place" (87).

Paul provided letters of reference for those he sent out for missionary service, but he did not apply this practice in his own travels. As Saul the Hebrew, he often used these commentary letters from the High Council as he traveled about, especially as he sought to eradicate the "cult" of Jesus followers. However, as Paul the convert of Christ he established a new practice that was entirely unique. Rather than being validated by a human system, Paul saw his worthiness for ministry emanating from God who provided all authority. In the holistic recreation of salvation and faith, one's worth and authenticity are to be found in the new movement. Yet once again, Paul's embracing of new practices created friction with the not-so-mature church in Corinth.

There is little doubt that the Corinthians had regressed spiritually over the long year between visits by Paul. For the most part, the second letter is one long defense against Corinthian accusations toward Paul. Paul was being accused of everything from being a charlatan to being in league with Satan. The citations against Paul seemed to increase as the Corinthians grew more dysfunctional.

As chapter 3 opens, Paul's audience seemed to want him to provide a letter of recommendation upon his return. Since both Corinthian letters are merely responses to questions and issues sent earlier to Paul, we have only his responses to study. It would be grand to have both the Corinthians' questions and Paul's response, but since the former no longer exist, we must make inferences from the words of Paul.

Despite the obvious attack upon his credibility, Paul responds in ways that shape and define the theology of recreation in Christ. Rather than respond in kind, which he sometimes did, Paul shifts the idea of letters of recommendation coming from human sources to the individual believer becoming a living reference. This is a major religious and social departure from the thought and practice of the era. In fact, this was on the level of many of Jesus' pronouncements that created the widening gulf between his teachings and those of entrenched Judaism. Paul was in effect redefining the total scope of Christian living for the Corinthians.

New Letters of the New Heart

The credibility attack upon Paul's worthiness to counsel the Corinthians was a genuine insult. Considering the preponderance of charlatans and more accomplished crooks among the numbers of traveling teachers, the suggestion that Paul needed credentials for a return visit was foul. One school of thought views these personal attacks as pointed more to Paul's perceived arrogance and practice of self-aggrandizement. A tone of "who do you think you are?" prevails in this section, but that mind-set could be supported by either stance since neither view lightens the obvious tension between the church starter and the church. Which issue is central in this debate really doesn't matter. Paul's response is the most important item to be found in these verses as it shifts the burden of authenticity from a reference letter penned by a person to the changed life of a person who has found salvation in Christ.

In 3:1, Paul inquires, "Surely we do not need, as some do, letters of recommendation to you or from you, do we?" The reality exists in this question either that Paul had been demeaned by the slight of the Corinthians suggestion that he provide credentials or that he was in some way praising himself with personal recommendations. In reality he needed neither a letter of reference nor to praise his own accomplishments. These verses speak about Paul the prolific church planter and evangelist. The attack upon his credibility was genuine and personal. So was his response, but not in the normal ways one imagines or expects.

Paul leaps over the personal insult and lays new theological ground with his response. In v. 2 he tells them they are the living letters of reference and authenticity of his ministry. Their changed lives and their new relationship with Christ provide for his credibility. This new type of reference letter is no longer written in ink, but supernaturally on the hearts of each and every believer.

> The imagery again is striking. Instead of something written on paper with pen and ink, he pictures a divine letter inscribed on human hearts by the spirit of the living God. The Corinthians are Paul's letter to the world; having been engraved on his heart, known and read by everyone . . . Paul's credentials are not on paper but in persons. (Garland, 157)

Paul uses v. 3 to focus on this new view of letters of recommendation being entirely supernatural. He states that the supernatural letter was based in Christ, with God as the author. This obviously lent great credibility to the new view as opposed to such letters being written by a person. Next he states that the new letter relates to and reflects upon his ministry. The Life Application Commentary lists Paul as being "inextricably intertwined" with the Corinthians (311). Truthfully stated, Paul was involved in their lives before Christ became the centerpiece. Paul personally led most of them to Christ, so they were indeed a testament to his ministry. Thirdly, the Holy Spirit was the actual inscriber of this letter and was God's spirit that indwelled each Corinthian believer. Paul concludes by stating again the huge contrast between a letter written in ink and one penned in and by the Spirit of God.

Not Exactly Written in Stone

Paul's next analogy centers on inscriptions cut into stone in contrast to those impressed upon the receptive hearts of humankind. The readers in Corinth would be knowledgeable of various laws, mottos, and validations chiseled into stone, as they were common throughout the Roman world. Jewish Christians would make quick reference to the Torah or Decalogue that formed the basis of Hebrew law as a guide for righteous living. Paul's message here may well have been that even the most esteemed words written in stone are merely inadequate, lifeless carvings. An inference that adds to Paul's words is simply this: a tradition is incapable of offering a response where a heart and soul not only offer, but also require, response. If we see this as the difference between ritualism and spirituality, we will move closer to Paul's likely intended vision.

Hafemann sees Paul's processes as being even larger than merely the movement from ritual practices to being spirit-based. In a much wider scope, Paul is drawing an even more distinct line between the old and new covenants. "While in the 'Old Age' the focus of God's activity and revelation was the law, in the 'New Age' according to Ezekiel, God will be at work in the heart" (221). He goes on to say that "Paul understands himself to be an eschatological agent of revelation though whom the Spirit is now being poured out in the Gospel" (224).

So now we have Christ portrayed as the foundational agent of salvation, righteousness, and faith to and for the Corinthians. This was a heavy theological issue for such a young congregation in such a young movement. Despite their lack of maturity, this message had to be presented at this time in their faith lives. Much like John's presentation of Jesus in his Fruit of the Vine discourse, a line of stark demarcation must be established between the old covenant and the new covenant.

When Paul cites the new covenant in v. 6, he effectively captures what Jesus taught in John 15:1 about superseding Israel and becoming the New Israel and the True Vine. Whereas in the time prior to Jesus one's salvation depended upon an identity with Israel, the path and focus had become new in all ways through Jesus. The long-term fruitlessness of Israel gave way to the new path to salvation and abundant living through the New Israel or the True Vine—Jesus, as portrayed in John 15.

It is important to note the unique Greek word translated as *new* in these verses, for it shifts the overall emphasis to a higher level. Too often the term *new* signifies nothing more than an updated version of an already existing item. The word translated in v. 6 into the catchall English *new* actually means a qualitatively original newness heretofore unknown. The move away from the spiritually distant Hebrews and their fruitlessness was indeed a move toward something new in every possible sense of the word. The arrangement between God and his people was now new. The expectations God had for his people were now new. The path to God's salvation was now new. The sum total of these new elements equals the new covenant. As Belleville put it, "What is qualitatively better about the New Covenant is that it is not a 'letter' Covenant—that is, an external code—but 'Spirit' Covenant—that is, an internal power . . . . Paul describes this elsewhere as a 'new self created' to be like God in true righteousness and holiness (Eph 4:24)" (94-95).

The New Glory of the New Covenant

Sadly many centuries had passed since the glory of God was made manifest in the old covenant. As people tend to do either because of the vagaries of human nature or the selfishness of the sin condition, Israel existed primarily in their past. They were quick to bring up Moses and focus on his encounter with God. The Hebrews were so individually woven into the fabric of performance-based law that the law itself had become synonymous with righteousness. Over time the path to salvation had drained all vestiges of relationship from their faith lives. The people had employed a form of regressive revelation that had rendered all revelation hollow, myopic, and void. They had allowed God's glorious covenant with them to die in ways eerily reminiscent of a drought-stricken vineyard slowly drying up from the roots.

Paul makes this distinction in 3:7-11, stating that the Moses covenant brought death and condemnation, whereas the new covenant in Christ brings life and righteousness. It is important at this point to understand fully the reasons for the demise of the earlier covenant. It is not that it was a flawed covenant from the inception, which it wasn't, nor should we suspect God's changing mood or direction. In plain and simple terms, Israel ceased being a holy nation and a nation of priests in order to become nationalistic and overly insulated. They began to despise the peoples God initially sent them to redeem. Pratt sees their main problem as being basic sin (324), which is likely the most central of all issues that led to their breaking the covenant with God and their failing as the chosen people (Jer 31:32).

Paul goes to great lengths to portray the stark contrast between the two covenants. By the end of this section, it is clear that the Hebrews had, over time, rendered the old covenant all but null and void. Paul cites the "faded glory" (3:8) as testament to the literal past tense of the former covenant and, more importantly, to the glory of the new arrangement. The new covenant brings righteousness, is housed in the heart and soul of each redeemed believer, and will last for eternity (3:9-11).

No longer would humankind rely on the labyrinth-like law to achieve salvation. Salvation would be found in personal relationship with Jesus Christ. No longer would living by faith be identified as living by the prescribed letters of the law. Faith living would be guided by the Spirit of God, which resides in each believer. No longer would God's covenant with the created peoples be subject to the whims of like individuals. Through Christ, the new covenant would be built in glory and power, all the while defeating the eternal power of sin and setting the stage for everlasting glory. New? Newer? Newest? All three signify the new path to salvation and righteousness and the hope for all people.

Life Lessons

The modern world still requires facsimiles of ancient letters of recommendation. In a world of resumes, background checks, and credit reports, there exists a written reputation on almost every adult. In some ways, we haven't changed a great deal since the inception of the new covenant. Nevertheless, the most important facet of our personal reputation should still be that of "person of faith." The new covenant should be written in our hearts and souls and made manifest by the profound differences evidenced in our lives. This may be why Paul used a Greek word of mixed meaning to describe what is essentially the "letter of recommendation" that is our life. He used *doxa* for *glorious* at a time when the same word was used secularly for *reputation*. Seen together, this can showcase a truly glorious reputation or way of life that is the point Paul tried to push across to the recalcitrant Corinthians.

It is important to not allow the fact that 2,000 years have passed since the new covenant surpassed the former one. In some ways, it is easy to argue that the new covenant isn't new at all, especially when viewed chronologically. Doing so, however, would repeat mistakes made by the Hebrews of the old covenant. Neither covenant should be seen in ways of definable time, nor should *new* be judged chronologically. The *new* for the Corinthians is the same *new* for people today: it is to be *new* in Christ and to live a *new* life in the Spirit.

> The Old Covenant suffers immeasurably from a comparison with the new. It belonged in fact to a varsity order, an economy that began to fade immediately after its inception, as was typified by the divine glory reflected on Moses' face—a glory that began to fade as soon as he left the divine presence. On the other hand, a Covenant destined to be permanent must be invested with a far greater glory. (Harris, 336)

This glory must be borne out in our lives if the new covenant has made us truly new.

1. Cite the difference between Paul's views on qualifications for ministry set by God versus those set by human beings.

_____

_____

_____

_____

_____

_____

2. Describe ways that the Corinthians had become Paul's ministry project, thus becoming his living letter of commendation.

_____

_____

_____

_____

_____

_____

3. Contrast the old covenant and the new covenant in relation to God's one overall plan for humankind.

_____

_____

_____

_____

_____

_____

4. How did the former covenant bring death as Paul states in vv. 7-8?

_____

_____

_____

_____

_____

_____

5. What does Paul mean in contrasting the fading glory of the old covenant with the surpassing glory to come?

_____

_____

_____

_____

_____

_____

6. Contrast Jesus as the agent of salvation, righteousness, and faith with avenues to those elements before Jesus.

_____

_____

_____

_____

_____

_____

7. Cite possible implications for today's church found in this chapter.

_____

_____

_____

_____

_____

_____

Genuinely Genuine

2 Corinthians 4

In the preceding chapter of his second letter to the Corinthian church, Paul laid claim to being a minister of the new covenant. In looking at the whole of Paul's life, this proclamation becomes both amazing and profound. One would be hard pressed to locate anyone else in history that came to Christianity from such a distance as Saul of Tarsus. Yet it is Paul—formerly Saul, the zealous Pharisee—who embodies and defines all that is meant by following Christ as Savior and Lord.

Saul was born in Tarsus, the capital of Cilicia, which in today's geography would be southern Turkey. Tarsus was a Roman city so fervent in its loyalty that during the reign of Julius Caesar it temporarily adopted the title Juliopolis. Tarsus was also the city where Antony first met Cleopatra, which occurred some thirty years before Saul was born. Tarsus was home to many varied Greek religions, including a flourishing worship of Herakles, thought of by many to be a divine savior. In addition, there was a healthy Jewish population in Tarsus during the time Saul would have been growing toward adulthood. Saul was educated in his faith in Tarsus and progressed to the upper levels of the rabbinical system there.

> It is believed Saul studied Judaism under the legendary Pharisee, Gamaliel. Over time Saul rose through the ranks of the rabbinical system and became a ranking Pharisee. It is also evident from the Book of Acts that Saul became a zealous persecutor of the Christian movement. Acts 9:1-3 portrays the High Priest authorizing Saul to go to the Synagogues in Damascus to bring back to Jerusalem Jews who had accepted Jesus. (Sanders, 10)

During this mission, Saul had an encounter with God that changed his life, his name, and history itself. Saul went through a complete transformation after this supernatural experience.

> Saul grapples with his dawning realization that his life, though lived in zeal for the one true God, even to the point of persecuting the church, has in reality been one of "ignorance in unbelief" (1 Tim 1:13). Through the question "why?" he begins to see that in proving his commitment to God by persecuting the church, he has actually been proving himself an enemy of God. As Saul deeply considers the "why?" and accepts the divine perspective on his actions, his whole spiritual world is turned upside down. What was gain will become loss (Phil 3:6-9). What was a badge of honor will become a lifelong shameful blot on his character (1 Cor 15:9; 1 Tim 1:13, 15). (Larkin, 139)

Though struck blind by his encounter, Saul follows the divine directions into the city, going without food or drink for three days. Much has been made of his blindness, which no doubt had more than mere symbolic purpose, especially to the recipient. At the very least, Saul's blindness reflected his own inherent spiritual blindness as to God's purposes and plans. Through this period, Saul merges into his new life in Christ. He "is" the new person that he will soon teach and preach the people to become in order to find genuine spiritual fulfillment. He becomes Paul, the message bearer to the Gentiles and defender of the faith.

Paul defining himself through the new covenant, then, is a natural outgrowth of his experiences with God dating from his days as a Pharisee. He has related to God from both sides and in both ways and knows with complete confidence that the glory of God has been made known through Christ. This reality fuels and empowers Paul's ministry.

Defense Exhibit A: The Ministry Defined

In this section Paul begins a defense of his ministry and his commitment to a flawless gospel. Paul was reacting to criticism from the Corinthians over his delayed visit. They had resorted to prior petty practices and questioned his motives and methods even to the point of suggesting deceit. No doubt the church had witnessed teachers who ministered more for personal gain than from a commitment to the gospel of Christ. There were false teachers aplenty at that time and abuses did occur. It is a natural human tendency to seek adulation, attention, and personal gain. Imagine how easy it would have been for someone of Paul's stature and obvious gifts to succumb to moments of base selfishness. But what happens to the message when the teacher misapplies judgment?

These negative realities seem to spur Paul's vigorous defense of his motivations for ministry. Paul also seemed to sense a need for the Corinthians to focus more on the message than on the messenger. The messenger is temporal and flawed while the message is ageless and uncorrupted. Focus for too long on the provider of the message and one will in time lose touch with the message. This could be why Paul used the illustration of "jars of clay" to signify that through which the message is proclaimed.

> The treasure however, is in jars of clay. The Gospel is the revelation of God. It is meant to do for the world what the creation of light did for the chaotic earth. But we ministers are to have none of the glory of the work. We are nothing. The whole power is of God. (Hodge, 69)

Paul recognized his limitation and knew that he was nothing without the power of God at work in his life. That realization would be beneficial for all believers, especially for those who seek to serve and live out their special calling. Rather than seeing limitations as a negative, Paul promoted his insufficiencies as part of his effective ministry. Through the realization that he lacked sufficient personal power or wisdom, Paul found his well of strength. Despite attacks from inside and outside the faith, Paul did not "lose heart" (v. 1) for his work as a minister. "From these verses we see that to 'lose heart' means at least two things: (1) Paul did not give in to the temptation to use deceit in his ministry, and (2) he did not crumble to the pressures of persecution and hardship" (Pratt, 334).

In the renewing strength of his calling, Paul renounced behavior that would have discredited the gospel and his ministry. The Corinthians were on the attack and had accused Paul of everything from tardiness to being a false teacher. Paul cited three inappropriate practices in these verses that frame his defense:

(1) *We have renounced the shameful things that one hides* (4:2). Paul was stating that no evil tactics or ulterior motives were in play in his

ministry. It is important to note that Paul was not suggesting that he was blameless or without shame. On the contrary, Paul's pre-Christian past must have been a weight of guilt always within reach. Rather than overstate his righteousness, Paul focused on his motivation for ministry. For Paul, ministry was an extension of God and therefore must be framed in holiness and purity. Any exercises in subterfuge for personal gain would be an affront to God.

(2) *We refuse to practice cunning.* . . (v. 2). The Greek word used here (*panourgia*) essentially means "trickery." "The accusation of trickery and deceit was commonly labeled against Sophists and certain philosophers of the day" (Hubbard, 43). Paul undoubtedly was trying to create space between his ministry and that of the philosopher and often-opportunistic itinerant preachers of the day. His statement implies much more than simply teaching as it relates to deception. *Use* is literally "to walk," a Greek verb that occurs frequently in Paul's writings to describe the Christian life. The term for "deception" means "capable of anything." "It often refers to those who use their ability unscrupulously and with cunning and slyness" (Belleville, 114). Paul is implying that ministry is as much the character and commitment of the messenger as it is the genuine message.

(3) . . . *or to falsify God's word* (v. 2). The accusation against Paul of playing free and easy with the message was the most common of all attacks. Paul's emphasis on the words of Christ cost him among those who either remained true to the Mosaic Law or overstated their freedom from the constraints of that law. Paul's attitudes covering the frailty of human wisdom never played well with educated Greeks, who also took issue with the reality of the resurrection. It is clear Paul saw the words of Christ as holding both ultimate power and truth. Any devaluation of these truths would render the message corrupted. Paul always stood on his integrity toward God's word.

Defense Exhibit B: The Enemy Defined

Paul begins the first Corinthian letter by citing the reality of interpersonal issues that were damaging the young church. "Now I appeal to you, brothers and sisters, in the name of our Lord Jesus Christ, that all of you be in agreement and that there may be no divisions among you" (1 Cor 1:10). In the following verse, he goes on to say he had been informed of quarrels among the fellowship, even to the point of picking sides over favorite teachers and leaders. As we move through the fourth chapter of the second letter, we find the Corinthians mounting an offensive against Paul, questioning his ethics and motives for ministry. It is obvious that the Corinthian believers had not made great spiritual progress over the long year between Paul's letters; in fact, one has to wonder if any substantial growth and maturity had taken place.

This obvious reality seems to prompt Paul to cite the influence of "the god of this world" (v. 4) as the negative root of all selfishness. While his citation was pointed primarily toward unbelievers, it is no coincidence that he uses it in his defense against charges of malfeasance by the Corinthian church. It is true that Satan works to veil the minds of unbelievers against the ultimate truth of God, as it is also true that instability within a church is often the work of evil. Satan had become in real ways "the one whom this age had made its god" (Harris, 340). Paul had respect for the danger of Satan's reach and influence, both within the struggling church and among his mission field. This mention of "the god of this age" was to be a serious warning to the church of a real and active enemy.

Defense Exhibit C: Respecting Adversity

Paul continues to defend his ministry by changing the direction and context of the discussion. To promote the centrality of God in both his life and his ministry, Paul details the difficult existence of a preacher and a teacher of the gospel. The treasure of God's redemptive gospel is transported in "clay jars" (v. 7), merely vessels of humanity prone to all of life's negatives. Paul seemed to have two primary lessons in mind in this section. First, God supplies any and all power for Paul and his associates to perform their ministry. To those who charged Paul with selfish motivation and personal gain, he has these words, "we are afflicted in every way, but not crushed; perplexed, but not driven to despair" (4:8). Since it is clear that Paul's life could be defined as one hardship after another, it is difficult to find evidence of any personal material gain.

Paul's second lesson gleaned from these verses focuses on the reality of God's power embodied in suffering. It is no secret that Paul and his associates had a rough life to that point. However, rather than allow his suffering to impede his ministry, Paul proclaimed that God becomes glorified through pain. Savage comments, "It is only in weakness that the power may be of God, that [Paul's] weakness in some sense actually serves as the ground for divine power" (166). Pratt adds, "To carry around the death of Christ was to suffer repeatedly for his glory. Even so, there was a purpose to his suffering" (339).

For Paul, suffering, persecution, and hardship were "to be expected" in serving Christ. Raised to another level, there was also evidence of the power of God in the lives of Paul and his associates: "For we were so utterly, unbearably crushed that we despaired of life itself. Indeed, we felt that we had received the sentence of death so that we would rely not on ourselves but on God who raises the dead." (1:8b-9).

Also, Paul's references to death were not to be seen in light of any finality, such as "this will be over soon and I can go home." Rather, they were linked to Christ's cross as its corollary, focusing more on the glory and power of the resurrection. Suffice it to say Paul saw victory, blessing, and power in personal hardship, with the ultimate outcome being God glorified.

Defense Exhibit D: Verdict on the Future

Paul transitions for the closing phase of his defense against the various Corinthians' accusations. Some scholars view this section as actually being post-defense, citing these verses as more theological teaching than argument. Whichever view is accepted, it is hard to escape the future implications found in these verses. Paul borrows heavily here from Psalm 116 as he describes a form of reciprocal adversity where service leads to hardship, which then leads to even more hardship and so on. This reality is presented to the Corinthians, but since this is repetitive and already known, Paul's intention must be something else entirely.

It is said that when the outcome of an endeavor is known and assured, a form of resignation sets in. One could see how that could lead either to paralysis of the spirit or complete surrender. In Paul's world, the total opposite was true. Paul voiced assurance that despite the adversity he would remain true to his calling and to his certainty of spending eternity with God. He cites the power of the death and resurrection of Jesus as proof positive that God will reward him at life's end. Christ died for God's kingdom, was resurrected and then ascended to heaven, setting the example for a post-death resurrection for believers who would spend eternity with God.

Paul speaks boldly because his faith reveals to him that beyond earthly tribulation lies the assurance that God will resurrect him. Those who belong to Christ and experience his living power in this life will also belong to him on the other side of death. . . . As Christ's death brought us life, so Christ's resurrection makes possible the life to come. (Garland, 235)

Lambrecht adds, "Paul's proclamation is grounded in his faith-certainty of a final outcome: his resurrection after death—firmly based on Christ's past resurrection—and what can be called a gathering forever of all Christians with Jesus in the presence of God" (348).

Paul wraps up his defense against accusations of ulterior motives for ministry by teaching the Corinthians about God's ultimate reward for faith. Leading up to this point, his focus had been on defining genuine faith through his ministry example. Simply put, to serve God is to have faith in God. One's faith is tested by adversity, but at the same time, one's faith is also defined by how he or she deals with adversity.

Life Lessons

At first glance it doesn't appear that 2 Corinthians 4 is instantly applicable to today's church. After all, its content is focused on Paul defending his ministry to a basically dysfunctional, selfish church.

However, a serious study of this chapter provides a wealth of healthy information beneficial to the new millennium church. The reality that many of today's churches remain dysfunctional and selfish cannot be overlooked. While the church of today is substantial and sophisticated in comparison to its earliest counterpart, at its essence little has changed. Would today's church give Paul a difficult time if the century were different? Chances are, it would. That probability is the greatest lesson to be gained from this section.

The Corinthian church lacked spiritual maturity and a basic heart for ministry. They were selfish and seemed to see only the smallest picture possible. Paul, however, speaks of a grander church, one in which selflessness triumphs over sin. His view of God's church is a fellowship of believers who love God to the point of being willing to lay down their lives for the cause. He describes a church of ministers who see the biggest of all possible pictures. He sought the church of his day to live with an expectancy of a future resurrection.

By Paul's scale, how is the church of today doing? Suffice it to say it is doing well with respect to persecution and hardship, but possibly not so well in other "Corinthian-like" areas. This chapter is much more than lessons in not seeking personal gain through faith. Through seeing the foibles of the Corinthian church, we gain our greatest insights. Simply put, whatever they were doing, do the extreme faith opposite. Then we might have a church Paul would be proud of.

1. Briefly describe the before-and-after story of Saul/Paul.

_____

_____

_____

_____

_____

_____

2. Explain how someone could become an enemy of God as referred to in this section.

_____

_____

_____

_____

_____

_____

3. Contrast Paul's definition of ministry with his analogy of jars of clay.

_____

_____

_____

_____

_____

_____

4. Identify ways in which trickery and distortion could be used today to damage a church.

_____

_____

_____

_____

_____

_____

5. Describe or define Satan as being the "god of this age" (2 Cor 4:4).

_____
_____
_____
_____
_____
_____

6. In what ways or for what reasons should suffering and persecution be expected in serving God?

_____
_____
_____
_____
_____
_____

7. Identify ways in which a spiritual future view can assist believers during times of suffering or persecution.

_____
_____
_____
_____
_____
_____

8. Identify ways in which today's church is "Corinthian-like."

_____
_____
_____
_____
_____

To cite Paul's relationship with the Corinthians as "love-hate" would certainly be an understatement. It is obvious Paul had an intense love (agape) for this church and these people. It is also obvious that they soured on Paul between visits and regressed spiritually over the months. This spiritual regression led to much dysfunction among the people and to general disorder within the church. Through all of this Paul became somewhat of a punching bag or whipping boy to the Corinthians. A psychologist might suggest they were transferring their spiritual discomfort to Paul in the form of accusations and complaints. This would be similar to "shooting the messenger" when the message wasn't well received, which in reality changes nothing of substance (except for the messenger of course).

The Corinthians had inner-spiritual problems that allowed them to turn against Paul and against the basics of faith in Christ. They were moving farther and farther away from their ideal and, consequentially, more toward gross dysfunction. Was their altered spirituality positive for the movement? Could their state of dysfunction promote the Kingdom of God and lead to additional people finding solutions? The answer to both questions is absolutely not! The Corinthians were simultaneously operating as their own worst enemies and against the progress of the Kingdom of God on earth.

Against this backdrop Paul continues his discourse with the church in Corinth. It is at once a pep talk, a reality check, and a teachable moment. It is an opportunity for the Corinthians to return to the path toward righteousness and God's plan for their lives. It is a time for the whole church to experience the supernatural reality of becoming "new" in Christ. In chapter 5, Paul primarily focuses on their lack of progress.

Out of Our Minds

Paul is writing to the backsliding church in Corinth seeking reconciliation on two fronts. Obviously he is seeking to restore his now strained relationship with them, which the church seems to resist at each turn. In an even larger way, he is attempting to shift them back to the point of spiritual reconciliation. Their cumulative regression is evident throughout the second letter and it is the crux of all their problems with Paul. A glaring and consistent reality of their regression is the fact that they had fallen sway to other teachers and philosophers. Flashy presentations and world-class letters of recommendation had all but replaced the earlier focus on Jesus and his teachings. Against this reality, Paul shapes his focus in this section.

Paul's defense against the lingering influences of non-Christian teachers is that of basic awe. It is an amazing approach when properly analyzed, as it concentrates the focus on God and not on human words. Is Paul admitting that he can't compete against the learned philosophers of the day in basic oratory? Possibly, but since it is evident Paul did not lack in confidence, it is more likely he was opting for good theology. Inspiring words can and do lead to change, but how much change and for how long? Paul's defense was based on the total and complete change brought by God, not temporary emotional surges that rise and fall with frequency.

Paul tells the Corinthians that he "fears the Lord," an Old Testament allusion that means to respect and hold in awe. Through this sacred reality, Paul attempts to persuade people of their need for God. It is, in effect, an evangelistic tool as well as a basis for loving God. The Corinthians were asking Paul to demonstrate his authority before citing instructions and providing teaching. He was being judged against the powerful prose of popular philosophers and teachers. His response was simple: we fear God and have been indelibly marked, so take pride in our new lives and allow us to continue to share with you the life-changing message of Christ.

This is a classic approach. God had permanently charged Paul and his associates, and that reality propels them into ministry. Another way to frame Paul's response could be: judge not a speaker by his words but by his character. Thomas à Kempis stated, "You can be certain of this: when the Day of Judgment comes, we shall not be asked what we have read, but what we have done. Not how well we have spoken, but how well we have lived" (Barnett, 277).

Paul was confident that he was in proper relationship with God and that his motivations were pure. He had hope that both of these were clear and plain to the Corinthians and that they would actually take pride in his genuineness. This unique use of *pride* should not be confused with other usages that connoted arrogance or self-conceit. Paul's use of the term had much more to do with joy and spiritual delight than anything negative. Pride in this case could lead to corporate support and to a massive turn toward the positive for the entire Corinthian church.

Easily Paul's most telling statement is found in v. 13: "For if we are beside ourselves, it is for God; if we are in our right mind, it is for you." This phrase is used in Mark 3:21 in describing the reactions of Jesus' family to his messianic claims and zeal, both of which were seen as deranged. Paul, however, uses the phrase in greatly positive ways as he describes his passion for pleasing God and for his all but myopic view of life ("for me to live is Christ and to die is gain").

To many people, Paul would have seemed deranged or at least quite different. Yet he was attempting to bring the Corinthians to a place of great abnormality in the greater social sense. Is he saying believers must be different from the average masses that have not yet found their purpose in God? Is he saying that to love God with one's entirety will lead to an "oddball" status? A comprehensive reading of the New Testament leads readers to answer both questions in the affirmative.

Paul cites the "newness" factor in Christ as the unique differentiator among people. He may have seemed "out of his mind" to many people, but to those genuinely in Christ, he was normally abnormal, which is positive in the sense of being distinctly Christian.

Salvation's Newness

Paul's next statement deals with his compulsion for ministry. To say Paul was single-minded in his approach to life would be a huge understatement. He states that he is compelled to pursue this course due to the love of Christ. Any compulsion, positive or negative, has a root cause or focus. For Paul, the compassionate love of Christ compels his life's service. This divine love played out through Christ is one of dual aspects, however, that does nothing but strengthen its importance.

Christ's love as demonstrated through the Passion episode provides a positive compulsion for allegiance and service, with the response being a returned love. Paul recommends his multifaceted compulsion for ministry to the Corinthians.

The next focus is on the intense commonality found in salvation. The Corinthians were a fractious lot, divided by many small issues that colored the greater reality of the church. It is also possible that a by-product of their spiritual regression was a return to the greatly human habit of judging other people on their earthly merits. The Hebrews made this same mistake as they grew to despise the very peoples God had called them to reach in order to fulfill God's purposes. To hate is an all-too-human quality just as to love unconditionally is from divine influence. For Paul to cite the death of Jesus in vv. 14-15 is to teach the Corinthians that through Christ's act of salvation all people must die spiritually in order to become new. New, of course, implies a holistic newness and transformed appetite for love over hate. Yet this newness can result only from following the example of Christ in spiritual death and resurrection. Christ died literally, and in so doing he provided the example to be followed by those who *die* to the natural self to be *reborn* as newly redeemed believers.

"Christ's submission to God's will was a supreme act of self-giving love" (Garland, 279). Paul centers his teaching on this example in an attempt to bring the Corinthians back around to the full measure of their earlier conversions. It is easy to see how important this point is in light of the myriad problems in the Corinthian church. The key is simply to cease living for one's self and to live for the sake of, and good of, the greater Kingdom of God. Where Paul states, "You should no longer live for yourself," he is describing the most elemental teaching of Jesus as to living the life of faith. The church, not Paul, strayed from this ideal, and the church needed to reaffirm the full salvation provision of Christ.

Judge sees the Corinthians as clinging to age-old Greek self-protection ideals in their relations with Paul at this point (763). Thus Paul would not only be going counter to human thought, but also against ingrained Greek practice and mindset. Despite the obstacles, however, Paul doesn't flinch; instead, he stands firm in his "new" theology. He calls upon the Corinthians to embrace the full salvation act, to symbolically die to their old lives, and to embrace God's full newness. Obviously to Paul, it is all about becoming new.

The New Order

The next big step for the Corinthians is to cease viewing all of life through the lens of the unredeemed world. In vv. 16-21 Paul describes a new, out-of-this-world way of viewing life, one in which all things are judged from the perspective of the divine rather than the temporary societal order prone to fickle manipulations. Hodge states it this way: "Such is the nature of the change that I have experienced through the apprehension of Christ's love, as just described (v. 16), that I no longer see or judge things from a worldly point of view" (113).

In the earthly, natural world, people often hate one another and normally think of themselves first and second. In this temporal world the rich and powerful often prosper, while the good and just are downtrodden. Does this make sense? Strangely, no, it doesn't make sense nor does it strike of any equity at all. So the bigger question is this—"Why were the Corinthians clinging to a flawed world order of inconsistency and inclusion and fallibility, while resisting the new order of equality, consistency and inclusion?"

Obviously Paul couldn't figure that one out either; thus he continues to reach out to the church. He all but says God's unconditional love makes absolutely no rational sense. For the Greek-minded Corinthians, all of this was a huge leap, but let us not forget that Paul is writing to believers. This letter was sent to backsliding Corinthians, not rank and file pagan Greeks. Since they've already made most of the big decisions necessary for faith, Paul is seeking more to reconcile them with their previous commitments.

So what are the main needs Paul is addressing in these verses? The primary need all but leaps out of his words and is directed to the worldly mindset still held by most of the Corinthian believers. It is obvious that what was holding the church back was their regressive habit of focusing more on the temporary present than on God's new order. Paul's answer for this nefarious practice? Reconciliation. In v. 20 he asks them to be reconciled to God.

What would spiritual reconciliation bring to the Corinthians at this point of their spiritual struggle? In simple terms it would stop the backsliding and regression and begin the movement back to God's purposes. It would lead to the forgiveness of sin and would allow for cleansing. Reconciliation would allow for an altered view of the world, opening the way for new mindsets. This would also allow for the positive product Paul sought earlier in this chapter and an amazing "oneness" that can only be achieved through Christ. In short, it would bring about new and improved Corinthian believers who would be in a position to make profound differences among the lost citizens of first century Corinth.

Life Lessons

If Paul was working overtime in his attempt to bring the Corinthians believers back around to a world of truly reconciled living, what would he say about today's church? Is the church of today in a demonstrably better shape than the church in first century Corinth? Are we "awe-inspired" servants who take positive pride in the changed state of redeemed lives? Is the proof and reality of our commitment to Christ evident in every facet of our lives? Are we compelled to serve Christ due to the unconditional love we've been shown? Can we really say we embody Paul's words in v. 17: "So if anyone is in Christ, there is a new creation: everything old has passed away; see, everything has become new!"?

Chapter 5 is an all-inclusive lesson on thinking new, acting new, and seeing things from a new perspective, all as a result of becoming new in Christ. If any of the permanent vestiges of the former natural person are in play, we have slipped into a form of Corinthian dysfunction.

It is all about being holistically new in Christ, because of Christ and for Christ. Read that sentence again, because it is the linchpin for the entire session. It is due to Christ that we have the opportunity to become new and for Christ that we should become new. Think of it as reconciliation with the God who purposed us to allow this event to be the jumping off point into a life of all things new.

Being a Corinthian was not necessarily a great thing then, and being "like" a Corinthian today is certainly not where our aim should be. It is much better to be "out of our minds" like Paul, or put another way, abnormally normal!

1. Identify possible reasons the Corinthian church turned against Paul between his visits.

_____
_____
_____
_____
_____
_____

2. Identify ways spiritual regression can damage both churches and individual Christians.

_____
_____
_____
_____
_____
_____

3. In what ways had the teaching of gifted secular teachers and philosophers interfered with the work of Paul?

_____
_____
_____
_____
_____
_____

4. Cite ways Paul defended his ministry and teachings against the perceived effectiveness of the secular teachers.

_____
_____
_____
_____
_____

5. Identify ways in which Paul taught the Corinthians to become "new" again.

_____

_____

_____

_____

_____

_____

6. In what ways did the Corinthian Christians' small and temporal worldview hinder the church's effectiveness?

_____

_____

_____

_____

_____

_____

7. In what ways was Paul "out of his mind" for both the faith and for the Corinthian Christians?

_____

_____

_____

_____

_____

_____

8. If today's believers were "abnormally normal," how would the church be affected?

_____

_____

_____

_____

10 Stewardship . . . Impaired?

2 Corinthians 9

Paul's odyssey of instruction to the Corinthian church moved to the arena of stewardship. His teaching covers the bulk of two chapters, with the focal points centering on the Jerusalem collection. Paul labored for many years soliciting funds to assist persecuted and poor Judean believers who had been severely affected by a decade of famine. As early as AD 46, Paul and Barnabas delivered contributions to the famine-strapped Christians in Antioch (Acts 11:29-30). The solicitation of "missions" funds carried forth for some ten years.

Paul's cultivation of contributions from widespread Christians created the first cooperative relief fund whereby Christians interceded for other Christians. From a study of Acts, it is clear that all established churches cooperated in this relief effort instigated by Paul. However, as could be assured from 2,000 years of hindsight, not all churches were as generous or zealous as others. Which brings us to the oft-dysfunctional Corinthians and Paul's teachings on stewardship.

Stewardship in Corinth

Earlier in his first letter to the Corinthian church (16:1-4), Paul had instructed them to systematically set aside money as a ministry offering for the poor and persecuted believers. "On the first day of every week, each of you is to put aside and save whatever extra you earn, so that collections need not be taken when I come" (1 Cor 16:2). Fast-forward one year to his words in the second letter and discover that his instructions were not followed to the letter. For reasons left unstated, the offering had not been set aside as requested and the possibility of the Corinthians defaulting on their promises was genuine. Knowing that he had given them a year to plan for this ministry offering and had already praised their zeal and spiritual generosity to other churches, Paul faced a dilemma.

Paul was surprisingly positive and upbeat in his response to the seemingly stewardship-impaired Corinthians. Rather than chastise them or heap guilt and shame, Paul chose effusive praise and confidence to motivate them to honor their prior commitments. Some have suggested that this amounted to classic reverse psychology and an attempt to manipulate stewardship participation though praise-induced guilt. It is obvious that early Christians had many of the same issues related to faith and money as believers do today. It seems that throughout history, money has been the single biggest obstacle to full freedom in Christ. Speaking of Christians, David Garland writes, "Most people subconsciously employ a kind of mental air defense system to deflect any appeals for money that their radar screen picks up as approaching their way" (401). Michael Durall takes this a step further, referring to the annual stewardship drive as "congregational root canal(s)" (6).

Despite the fact that the Corinthians had cooled in their initial zeal to provide financial support to the strapped believers in Jerusalem, Paul voiced confidence that they would follow through on their commitments. He went as far as to say that if they did not follow through it would be a bad reflection on his ministry. This no doubt illuminated the true Kingdom nature of their commitment to provide assistance funds. In his own unique manner, Paul was teaching that stewardship is truly Kingdom-oriented and is much larger than either individual believers or churches. The scope and scale of stewardship is impossible to measure since it encompasses the entirety of God's work. How else could a comfortable Corinthian Christian assist a poor, persecuted believer in Jerusalem who was living though a famine?

Stewardship 101

The suddenly positive Paul followed with teaching that summarily lays out all of the benefits of Christian stewardship. He utilizes a common agricultural proverb, which teaches that sowing seed sparingly will result in a poor harvest and correspondingly sowing generous seed will later result in a bountiful harvest.

While Corinth was not an agricultural center, the symbolism would not have been lost on those of the mid-first century. The teaching is simply this: giving (sowing) generously will result at a later time in blessings (harvest). There is a genuine reciprocal relationship between positive stewardship and future blessings.

Paul's next statement applies to the intent and mindset of the gift. People give to God for many reasons, not all of which are positive. Some give from a deep-seated love that allows God to be more important than money. Others, sadly, give out of duty, framed more by guilt or legalism than love. Fear that bad things will occur if gifts are not made is also prevalent, although that approach seems absolutely pagan in contrast to the New Testament.

The clarity of promises in vv. 6-11 is unmistakably positive. If a Christian gives generously with the right spirit, God will bestow abundant reward.

> The rule of divine recompense that was the basis for giving in 9:6 is restated as a matter of principle in 9:7c: God rewards those who because they belong to the new covenant in Christ, give freely and generously, "for God loves a cheerful giver." Put negatively, there is no divine approval for giving to others merely out of duty. Instead, obedience, in order to count before God, must flow from a happy reliance on, and contentment in, God's gracious gifts to his people. (Hafemann, 367)

Paul was no doubt greatly influenced by the Hebrew texts, especially Proverbs 22:9: "Those who are generous are blessed, for they share their bread with the poor." The idea that generosity to those in need would result in personal blessing was common to Hebrew thought. However, the Corinthian church had been influenced to a great extent by the Greek philosophy of self-reliance. This mind-set obviously would lead to a much more narrow ministry worldview and more focus on the individual than the greater group. Where the basic Greek motive for giving was to show personal moral superiority, the Christian gave to glorify God and to progress God's Kingdom.

The Return on Investment

In the world of finance there is a basic concept of return on investment whereby all investments are evaluated in light of their return. If an investment shows a positive increase in its return, the investment is a success. The opposite would also be true whereby a negative return on an investment would render the investment a failure. Paul seems to say that there is no such thing as a bad investment (unless it is given through wrong motive). If a believer gives with proper heart and mind, a blessed return is guaranteed.

> One way God's approval of the cheerful giver (v. 7b) finds expression is in the provision of both spiritual grace and material prosperity (*all grace*) that will enable him constantly and generously to dispense spiritual and material benefits ("*you will abound in every good work,*" v. 8). As regularly as the resources of the cheerful giver are taxed by his generous giving, they are replenished by divine grace. This gives him a "Complete self-sufficiency" (*All that you need*) born of dependence on an all-sufficient God. (Harris, 376)

A question that has existed as long as Paul's writings centers on the exact form of these guaranteed blessings. It is possible Paul is guaranteeing an actual financial blessing in return for proper stewardship practice? After all, v. 11 does state, "You will be enriched in every way for your great generosity." The truth is, this section identifies tangible financial or material gain or supply of spiritual blessings. It could be assumed that in some cases, the return is tangible and "green," while in others it is entirely supernatural and spiritual. To speculate too much in either direction would seem to limit God, and these verses certainly portray God as truly limitless.

Caution must be applied lest a major point be missed. Paul is indeed stating that properly motivated stewardship will reap certain blessings. However, he is also stating that these blessings are to be applied with even greater generosity in the future. "Some commentators therefore interpret (these verses) to mean that God supplies the generous person with multiplied material blessings, so that, content as he himself is in every circumstances (cf. Phil 4:11), he may be able to shower multiplied benefits of every kind on the needy" (Harris, 376). If this is correct interpretation of the text, enhanced material blessings must lead to even more generous giving!

There Is No Bottom Line

In the world of high finance, there are, as you would expect, winners and losers. Sadly, the line between winning and losing is quite wide and it is normally an either-or proposition. This is anything but the case in God's economy of stewardship. If stewardship is properly practiced, there are absolutely no losers. Verse 11 sums up the escalating positives of cheerful and generous giving: "You will be made rich in every way so that you can be generous on every occasion, and through us your generosity will result in thanksgiving to God."

This final section provides insight into the enormous scope that stewardship encompasses. It is almost trite to cite a gift that "keeps on giving," but that's exactly what proper stewardship becomes. The final few words of v. 9 state that "his righteousness endures forever." While some interpret this phrase to mean that generosity is "never forgotten," it could mean the effect "never stops." The latter view meshes well with vv. 10-15 as we see the benefits of generous giving demonstrated.

Linda Belleville details the various beneficiaries of proper stewardship in this last portion of chapter 13:

• The giver (vv. 10-11)
• The recipients (v. 12)
• God (vv. 11-12)
• The church (vv. 13-14) (237)

Stewardship exercised with willingness and generosity will have both inclusive and long-term effects. The individual giver will be rewarded with blessings, either spiritual or material, and will be different due to the experience. Those who are assisted by the generosity of someone else will see and feel life change in unique ways. God will be exalted and glorified in both directions and the Kingdom will be made stronger. Finally, the church will mature, increase in multiple ways, and see spiritual gain. It is a genuinely win, win, win, and keep winning proposition. This is what Paul labored to communicate to the Corinthian church at its obvious teachable moment.

Paul sums up his lengthy teaching session on giving with a statement that brings the concept back to its point of origin: "Thanks be to God for his indescribable gift!" (2 Cor 9:15).

God is the original source of all we see and possess, thus God has already modeled stewardship for us. The full scope of God's provisioning is truly "indescribable" and is best honored by emulating as best we can. For both the mid-first century Corinthians and today's believers, stewardship is the best way to honor and emulate the gifts of God. "The source of all this is the ability to give, the desire to give, the reconciliation that would occur . . . was solely from God's hands. God is the ultimate Giver" (Osborne, 411).

Life Lessons

The implications of Paul's teaching on generous giving are as applicable today as they were to the early church. In fact, one could argue that the church in general has not progressed to any great degree in this area throughout history. The reality provided by numerical summaries is sad when stewardship practices are studied. They show a modern church filled with fewer and fewer tithers and others who give proportionally smaller amounts each year.

According to the Generous Giving website (www.generousgiving.org), one of every twelve adults practices tithing; there has been a steady decline in the percentage of givers, down 6 to 8 percent each year from 1998 to 2000; In 2000, 17 percent of Americans claimed to have tithed, while only 6 percent did so; Americans made collectively $7.51 trillion in 2000 and gave $152 billion. According to recent studies, Americans could have doubled their giving to $320 billion without any changes in lifestyle; furthermore, the more money a person makes, the less likely they are to give.

It is clear that Paul's words to the stewardship-impaired Corinthians have enormous application to the church today. Truth be told, the Corinthians actually look good in comparison to the sad state of giving practices in place today. Yet, the same truths hold firm for the twenty-first century as it did for the first. God expects cheerful and generous giving. God rewards proper giving with bountiful blessings, both materially and spiritually. The Kingdom of God is expanded, enhanced, and empowered by proper stewardship. Everyone wins! Unless, of course, we continue to ignore the true path to success in both faith and life.

1. How does the basic concept of the tithe mesh with Paul's words in 1 Corinthians 6:2?

_____
_____
_____
_____
_____
_____

2. Identify factors that allow believers to compromise, even default, on their stewardship obligations.

_____
_____
_____
_____
_____
_____

3. Identify reasons why some view the annual stewardship emphasis as "congregational root canal" (Durall).

_____
_____
_____
_____
_____
_____

4. The average Corinthian believer was better off than the objects of the offering for poor, famine-strapped Christians elsewhere. Identify ways that wealth could hinder stewardship practices.

_____
_____
_____
_____

Stewardship . . . Impaired?

5. Second Corinthians 6:11 suggests rewards for generous giving from a right spirit. Describe possible rewards.

_____

_____

_____

_____

_____

6. Identify ways in which a person could give for the wrong reason(s).

_____

_____

_____

_____

_____

7. Describe how the following might be beneficiaries of generous giving:
• Giver
• Recipients
• God
• Church

_____

_____

_____

_____

_____

8. How would you describe generous giving?

_____

_____

_____

_____

Bibliography

Barnett, P. *The Second Epistle to the Corinthians*. Grand Rapids MI: Eerdmans, 1977.

Barrett, C. K. *First Epistle to the Corinthians*. London: A. C. Black, 1971.

Belleville, Linda L. "2 Corinthians," *The IVP Commentary*. Downers Grove IL: InterVarsity Press, 1996.

Blomberg, Craig. *The NIV Application Commentary 1 Corinthians*. Grand Rapids MI: 1994.

Claman, Henry N. *Jewish Images in the Christian Church*. Macon GA: Mercer University Press, 2000.

Coleman, Lyman & Reace, Richard. *1 Corinthians*. Littleton CO: Serendipity House, 1988.

Craig, C.T. *First Corinthians*. Interpreter's Bible Series. New York: Abington Press, 1953.

Dunn James D. G. *1 Corinthians*. Sheffield: Sheffield Academic Press, 1995.

Durall, Michael. "Why Stewardship Is a Constant Struggle," *Net Results*.

Lubbock TX: Net Results November-December, 2001.

Fee, Gordon D. *The First Epistle to the Corinthians*. Grand Rapids MI : Eerdmans, 1987.

Fisk, Bruce. *First Corinthians*. Louisville KY: Geneva Press, 1998,

Furnish, Victor Paul. *The Theology of the First Letter to the Corinthians*. Cambridge UK: Cambridge Press, 1999.

Gaebelein, *Frank Expositor's Bible Commentary—Roman Galatians.* Grand Rapids MI: Zondervan 1976.

Garland, David E. *The New American Commentary: 2 Corinthians.* Nashville: Broadman, 1999.

Hafemann, S. J. *Suffering and Ministry in the Spirit—Paul's Defense of his Ministry in 2 Corinthians.* Grand Rapids MI: Eerdmans, 1990.

———. *The NIV Application Commentary on 2 Corinthians.* Grand Rapids MI: Zondervan, 2000.

Harris, Murray J. *The Expositor's Bible Commentary, Romans–Galatians.* Grand Rapids MI: Zondervan, 1976).

Hodge, Charles. *First Corinthians.* Nottingham: Crossway Books, 1995.

Judge, E. "St Paul as a Radical Critical of Society." *Interchange* 16 (1974).

Lambrecht, J. *The Eschatological Outlook in 2 Corinthians 4:7-15 in Studies on 2 Corinthians.* Leuven: University Press, 1994.

Larkin, William J. *Acts,* Downers Grove IL: InterVarsity Press, 1995.

O'Connor, Jerome-Murphy. *1 Corinthians.* Glasgow: Bible Reading Fellowship, 1997.

Osborne, Grant. *Application Bible Commentary, 1 & 2 Corinthians.* Wheaton IL: Tyndale, 1999.

Pratt, Richard L. *I & II Corinthians.* Nashville: Holman, 2000.

Talbert, Charles H. *Reading Corinthians.* Macon GA: Smyth & Helwys, 2002.

Romacher, Earl, & H. Wayne House. *Nelson's Teachers Resource on First Corinthians.* Nashville: Thomas Nelson, 2002.

Sanders, E. P. Paula. *Very Short Introduction.* Oxford UK: Oxford University Press, 1991.

Watson, Nigel. *The First Epistle to the Corinthians.* London: Epworth, 1992.